THE SWISS BANKING HANDBOOK
A Complete Manual for Practical Investors

BY ROBERT ROETHENMUND

BOOKS IN FOCUS INC., NEW YORK

DEDICATION

For my father who, as always,
provided support, instruction and inspiration.

Manufactured in the United States of America

Library of Congress catalog card number: 79-55800

ISBN: 0-916728-331

Books In Focus, Inc.
P.O. Box 3481
Grand Central Station
New York, N.Y. 10017

TABLE OF CONTENTS

FOREWORD

Swiss banking is a controversial subject; but rarely is it talked or written about with any real insight or understanding. Finally, a Swiss, who knows banking and understands the informational needs of the English-speaking world, has written the needed book on Swiss banking.

To the sophisticated business person, as well as the generally interested reader, there is still much mystery about Swiss banking. This book eliminates the mystery. Chapter by chapter, questions are answered; creating a total comprehension of the inter-workings of Swiss legal and financial systems.

Robert Roethenmund has provided a great service to the Swiss and their international banking customers. He has explained the true nature of Swiss thinking which is the key to understanding this unique country. The interesting cultural settings with which he traces the origins and development of Swiss banking do more than any other book I am aware of to tell readers exactly why the Swiss are as competent as they are.

Mr. Roethenmund, as a student of history and of banking, has molded the traditions and practicalities of Swiss banking into a handbook that tells you why Swiss banking will remain as one of the very best systems of financial services in the world. This book takes you inside the banks themselves, allowing you to learn the best and most efficient methods of doing business and banking in Switzerland.

By carefully defining Swiss value systems, Mr. Roethenmund provides readers with unusual information heretofore unavailable; information that is particularly helpful in creating successful personal as well as business relations with the Swiss.

There may be a few Swiss in official positions who will not approve of portions of this book. This is because Mr. Roethenmund tells of the inner workings and procedures that the Swiss utilize for making monetary and political decisions. These are the decisions that affect the monetary stability and thus the political stability of much of the free world. But I feel that such information can do nothing but be helpful in calling attention to the ability and responsibility that the Swiss apply to such important matters. In some ways, those of us in other countries are a little better off than we think.

After reading this book, you will "know" the Swiss in a very real and personal way. You will have a secure grasp of Swiss systems, and most important, be equipped to utilize them for your own benefit and protection.

As inflation accelerates in most parts of the world and political crises threaten the stability and economic security of civilized society, knowing how to work with the Swiss can be vitally important to our individual liberties and financial security. Robert Roethenmund, (with the possible except of his father, Otto), knows how this is done better than anyone I know. This book is excellent!

> **Nicholas L. Deak,**
> **Chairman,**
> **Deak-Perera Group**

PART 1
INTRODUCTION:

The History and Tradition of Swiss Finance

Switzerland through the looking glass.

A view of Swiss history and the roots of the banking industry ... mercenaries on the battlefield . . . and in international finance . . . The beginnings of banking secrecy and the growth of the banking sector . . . The importance of cantonal sovereignty and financial interdependence . . . internal strife in the seventeenth and eighteenth centuries . . . neutrality as a cornerstone for development . . . surviving the world wars.

Introduction

Imagine a world in which no country like Switzerland exists. A major arbitration center for the world's political and economic dealings would be lost. A sanctuary for those who had dared to challenge the authority of their governments would cease to exist. Neutrality as a political concept would have less meaning for most nations and far less viability as a political course during conflict. The efficient maintenance of international payments would suffer.

On the other hand, the laundering of illicit funds for corruption or bribery would be greatly curtailed. It would be easier to keep exchange rates in line in a world in which "Swiss speculators" would not be able to interfere in the market. Autocratic governments would be pleased that they could now more closely monitor their citizens' financial transactions worldwide.

Unquestionably, a world without a Switzerland would considerably complicate the lives of many, while simplifying regulation and surveillance by governments. The fact that Switzerland does exist is proof that people, and governments, have a need for it, where it is and as it is. The Swiss have a saying: "If there were not a country like Switzerland, one would have to be created." This may be somewhat of a pompous attitude but it illustrates well the central role that the Swiss see themselves playing in the world. The Swiss would like to imagine themselves as a people with a steady and strong foundation set in the midst of an ocean of troubles.

To comprehend that outlook a foreigner must regard Switzerland through a long range perspective. We may all have a tendency to become too complacent about our socioeconomic conditions if things are going more or less well from day to day. It is not until we have experienced the fear of political instability or the threat of government controls that we can truly appreciate the uniqueness of Swiss society. The Swiss have had to deal with repression and external intervention for centuries before being able to create an independent niche for themselves. In some countries like the United States such problems are only being encountered for the first time.

Make no mistake, though, Switzerland is by no means sacred, but it has managed to survive. By mediation and compromise Switzerland has survived insurrection, foreign conquest, and world wars. The geography and history of Switzerland have made the Swiss well suited to this role and their adaptability to changing political conditions has preserved their autonomy for them.

Whether by good fortune or concentrated effort, they have somehow been able to bypass much of the chaos that has struck Europe over the past few centuries. It is not surprising, then, that today's Switzerland can be admired as a haven or despised as being mercenary. Certainly there is a considerable amount of reality behind either perspective.

If you are going to be doing business in Switzerland it is worthwhile to know more about the people, how they think, their character, heritage and politics. Just as a mechanical clock cannot function without its fly wheels, neither can Switzerland function without the Swiss.

Switzerland through the looking glass

On August 1 of each year, we Swiss celebrate our national holiday. It recalls the founding of the Swiss confederation in 1291. The people of three rural communities had grouped together in the Rütli valley to form a confederation dedicated to protecting their common interests. It was a small gesture but would later prove to be more significant than anticipated when highlighted against the backdrop of turmoil and autocracy in Europe.

Back in the thirteenth century the St. Gotthard pass was first opened, and literally paved the way for commerce between the two great centers of European trade, Flanders and Lombardy. The importance of the route was duly noted by those in power and it was inevitable that they contested who had control over the pass and its access routes. The communities living along this North South mountain passage suddenly found themselves the center of much interest. Although the peasants in this area had long been subjugated to foreign rulership, the foreign rule had seldom ever exercised any control over this region. This in large part was due to the fact that this area was never considered very important because of its lack of natural resources and scarce population. This indulgent attitude on the part of foreign rulers was soon to change however.

The Emperor of Austria, Rudolph von Habsburg, was quick to recognize the importance of these valley communities vis-à-vis the St. Gotthard pass and he moved, after his coronation in 1273, to consolidate his power over these areas. It is an interesting historical aside to note that Rudolph von Habsburg may have also had particular interest in this area that is now Switzerland as his ancestral home, the Habichtsburg, is located not too far from central Switzerland.

Challenged by the encroaching rule of the Emperor Rudolph, the three communities, Uri, Schwyz, and Nidwalden, formed a secret alliance to preserve their liberty. It is this alliance that we commemorate on our national holiday every August first. Quite fortunately for the early confederation, Rudolph died before he could openly challenge them. They seized the opportunity offered by his death to openly announce their alliance in 1291.

In this, The Treaty of Everlasting Alliance, the first three members of what would gradually evolve into the Swiss confederation proclaimed:

" ... to aid and defend each other with all their power, with their lives and property, both within and without their boundaries, each at his own expense, against every enemy— whoever shall attempt to molest them ..."

"to accept no judge in our valleys who shall have obtained his office for a price, or who is not a native or resident among us ..."

"to uphold the law ... punish murderers ... and banish those who would screen (criminals) ... "

The treaty made it clear that these people had had enough of alien administrations and that they were determined to uphold the law and organize their social order for themselves.

There is a well known story about a Swiss named William Tell, which is said to have occurred shortly after the signing of this alliance. We have little historical evidence to support this legend, but that is not the important point. What is important is that William Tell exemplified the ideal of the strong willed, righteous-minded individual who made up the small peasant communities that dared to challenge the Emperor. Men like Tell exploited the situation to assert their independence and put their communities on the road to Swiss confederation.

As time progressed, the confederation, which at first was only three small communities, gradually gathered strength and they were able to successfully challenge the Habsburg rights to their land. In 1332 the first town entered the confederation, the town of Lucerne. Shortly thereafter to follow were Zürich, Zug, Glarus and Bern. By the end of the 14th century the core of Switzerland had been formed.

As the confederation grew in size, so too did the number of problems it had to face. In 1386 Leopold von Habsburg laid seige to Sempach, a town under the control of Lucerne, and in 1388 the Habsburgs also attempted to reconquer Glarus. Even though they were outnumbered in both cases the Swiss amazingly were able to pull through and even secure further victories against the Habsburgs. The peoples' army of the Swiss confederation turned out to be a tougher opponent than its enemies had expected. The Swiss gained considerable confidence; so much so that by the beginning of the 15th century they became brash enough to turn the tables on the Habsburgs and ventured to expand Swiss territory further. They moved northwards and occupied Jura, Thurgau, Aargau and later attacked southwards towards Italy across the Ticino.

As the Swiss continued to push their borders outward the rest of Europe began to cast an anxious eye on their progress. In 1499 the Swabian League, a group of South German towns, joined the Austrian Emperor Maximillian I to oppose further Swiss expansion. Opposing them were three eastern Swiss communities, two of which even spoke different languages. After a nine month war, the Swiss won a decisive victory and were not only able as victors to extend their territory but also gained acclamation for their

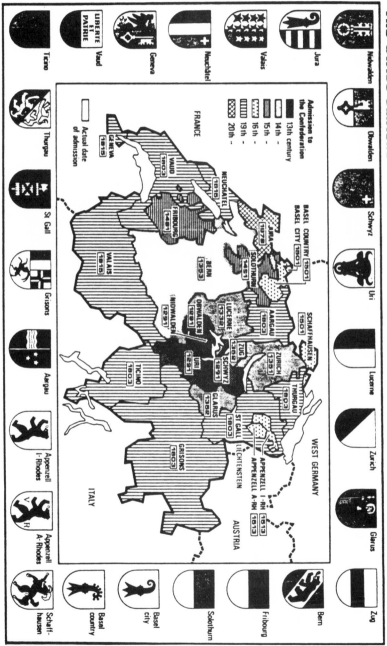

The Swiss cantons

Admission to the Confederation
13th century
14th -
15th -
16th -
19th -
20th -

Actual date of admission

Nidwalden, Obwalden, Schwyz, Uri, Lucerne, Zürich, Glarus, Zug, Bern, Fribourg, Solothurn, Basel city, Basel country, Schaffhausen, Appenzell A-Rhodes, Appenzell I-Rhodes, Aargau, Grisons, St Gall, Thurgau, Ticino, Vaud, Geneva, Neuchâtel, Valais, Jura fighting forces.

It was not long before some of the European rulers realized it would be far better to employ the Swiss as their soldiers than to have to worry about their warlike tendencies. The Swiss in turn were quite eager to serve as mercenaries. At home with few resources it was often hard to make a living, but by offering themselves to the highest bidders they could make a good living fighting abroad. So it was that the Swiss soldier came to be a prized asset for the royalty in Europe. The Swiss soldier was reliable, brave and trustworthy; all for a price. Over the three centuries from 1500 to 1800 literally millions of Swiss served as mercenary soldiers in France, Spain, Germany, Holland and Austria.

Unfortunately there were to be many tragic encounters during this period with Swiss fighting Swiss on foreign battlefields and in one case a mercenary Swiss army was even directed to attack its own country! It also led to much internal strife within Switzerland as certain cantons would agree to send troops to one side in a conflict while another canton would provide soldiers for the opposing side. Among the cantons animosity grew as soldiers from one canton would find themselves battling troops from a neighboring canton.

This was indicative of the type of decentralized government and sense of independence which the cantons felt and to a large degree still maintain today. Do not be surprised to find that the school system varies from canton to canton in Switzerland. That it may be nearly impossible to move into another canton because your child may not fit into the school system. Nor should it be surprising that even during government debates the representatives from the various cantons will speak only in the language of their canton. Though they easily understand each other in public they would be loathe to speak a language used by "another" canton. Each member of the confederation enjoys a wide margin of sovereignty. The foundations of the confederation were built upon this cornerstone of cantonal sovereignty.

Each canton basically governs itself and only appeals to the confederation for aid or support when the economies of scale warrant it. For this reason Switzerland never grew to be a great European power. Never could enough power be centralized to create an autocratic rule. Likewise this lack of autocratic rule is also responsible for Switzerland having been able to establish itself as neutral territory in the midst of its warlike neighbors. The Swiss passed up their chance to participate in an empire and opted for security on a small scale instead.

The apparent reversal in Swiss imperialism was not however solely prompted by the effectiveness of Swiss federalism. The Reformation was also very much a part of Swiss history during this formative period. No doubt the influence of men like Erasmus, Luther, Zwingli and Calvin made the Swiss much more introspective and less interested in further aggrandizement.

The Reformation caught on rather quickly among the Swiss population. The enlightened artisans and peasantry who made up the Swiss population had long been disillusioned by the wealth of the church and the corruption amongst much of its clergy. The Swiss had always been wealth conscious as a result of their lack of resources. Few were happy with a situation in which what little they had was being appropriated by the church.

It is also important to recognize that Renaissance ideas were quick to spread into Switzerland. They were brought in by many of the Swiss who had served in mercenary armies abroad, and also by the influence of great thinkers of the time like Erasmus and Calvin who were attracted to Switzerland by the tolerance of its government.

There were also great Swiss reformers too. Perhaps the best known of these reformers was Ulrich Zwingli (1484-1531). A man devoted to Christianity and motivated by humanism, he set out at an early age to transform Christianity in Switzerland not only by his words, but also by his deeds. His sermons were decidedly political in their message. He urged his congregation to condemn mercenary military service and he also commanded them to respect the local authorities who "were responsible for ensuring that justice was done on earth" - this tack made him very popular with the local government, which in turn was quick to give him more support.

Zwingli was also a great advocate of those two most holy of all Swiss traits: thriftiness and hard work. Zwingli firmly believed that through hard work and prayer a man could lead a good life, so long as he was not hemmed in by artificial restraints imposed by a temporal social order. His message had great approval among the peasant population who were eager to secure more liberty.

The success of Zwingli's reform movement was rapid. From his pulpit in the Grossmünster in Zürich he brought the Reformation not only to the citizens of Zürich but also to the citizens of many of the neighboring northern cantons. Zwingli's success lies largely in his ability to combine religious significance with political expediency, but mixing the two elements of religion and politics would also eventually lead to his downfall. Although the local government in Zürich was immensely pleased with Zwingli and quick to heap honor upon him, the governments in the other cantons were wary of his success as they did not like to see one man gather so much power.

In fact, they were not entirely wrong, as it probably was Zwingli's aim to have Zürich, maybe along with Bern, unite the confederation as a Protestant state.

The Catholic cantons to the South, however, would not stand for this and in 1529, along with Ferdinand of Austria, they formed a Catholic Union. The battle lines were drawn. It now seemed like only a matter of time before the Swiss confederation would be drawn into civil war. Religious dissension was threatening to bring about the disembodiment of the confederation.

Somewhat surprisingly, though, this was not at all the final outcome. there was a battle, a brief one, in which the Catholic cantons attacked Zürich, and in the ensuing fight Zwingli was killed. An uneasy peace was established in the aftermath of this battle as Protestant and Catholic cantons resumed their coexistence in a loosely bound confederation. The coexistence was not always on the best of terms. But whenever they were threatened by their European neighbors the members of the confederation would act as a unit to repel any aggression and dissuade foreigners from trying to intervene in any of Switzerland's domestic affairs.

It is also worth noting that Switzerland, though itself religiously divided, managed not only to remain neutral throughout the Thirty Year's War, but also was able to avoid any devastating civil conflict within its own borders.

The confederation was able to survive because the cantons

were determined to preserve their self-determination. They had no wish to be subject to autocratic rule, whether it came from within Switzerland or from outside. There were problems between the stronger cantons continually as one or the other sought to dominate. But one could never gather enough support to establish itself as a central power. Absolutism could not gain a foothold in Switzerland despite the fact that the social order was still largely based on the old feudal system. The only symbol of centralization existing was the Diet in Bern to which all cantons sent representatives. If anything was to be done involving two or more cantons it was done by common agreement, an agreement termed a gentlemen's agreement as there were no specific sanctions binding the parties involved apart from their good will. The modern day banking system in Switzerland has developed a system of internal control also based on such gentlemen's agreements. Their effectiveness is beyond dispute and, just like the old gentlemen's agreements between cantons, they are arrived at by common consent and enforced by the code of honor.

The Confederation ran quite well during this period considering there was no federal law, no national army and no national treasury. Historians consider this period as one of social and political stagnation in Switzerland but economically the first inroads were being laid to make Switzerland economically viable. As artisans and traders were forced to look abroad for their income Swiss "banking" was to lay its foundations. As early as the Thirty Years' War: "From His Imperial Majesty in Vienna and the Kings of France and England to the smallest German principality ... every governing authority was in debt to the cantons and towns of Switzerland."[1] In this period the banking industry began to evolve as one of the chief proponents of economic growth and stability in Switzerland. All during the seventeenth and early eighteenth century Swiss money lenders and tradesmen were integrating Switzerland into the world economy by providing foreign governments with long term financing.

When we speak of banking here we must realize that this is not banking in the modern sense of receiving deposits for safe keeping and then making investments in loans and bonds; rather banking before the nineteenth century consisted of raising capital and providing financial services such as foreign money exchange. In Basel, for example, the first forms of banking can be traced back to the fifteenth century. Already in the Middle Ages Basel had begun developing as an economic center for a large region. Located on the Rhine and bordering on France and Germany, Basel was a natural meeting place for itinerant merchants from all over the continent. Trading companies and international fairs were an ever present feature on the Basel scene. By the sixteenth century Basel was recognized as one of the major cities in Europe. Everything from saffarin to silk was traded through Basel. The city literally became a bastion of capitalism in Europe.

To meet the needs of the international clientele doing business in Basel foreign exchange houses began to spring up. In 1533 even the local city government became involved when they set up a public agency (Die Stadtwechsel Bank) to exchange foreign currencies. There were also a large number of merchant bankers who worked in foreign exchange houses or with one of the many trading firms. They were well acquainted with the commodity trade in Basel and they provided many of the services needed to support the local trader. Most of these merchant bankers were opposed to having the government become involved in their financial dealings. By 1746 they had proved their superior business sense when the government-run bank was forced to declare bankruptcy after a series of poor credit transactions.

Meanwhile, in other Swiss cities, the first seeds of the banking industry were also being sown. In Geneva, for example, during the War of the Spanish Succession a number of individuals acted as intermediaries between local money lenders and the King of France, Louis XIV. These middle men would typically obtain money at interest rates of between 7 and 10% and then lend these same funds out to the French at rates of up to 35%. Although the exact sums of money that Geneva provided Louis XIV are still unknown, it is estimated that nearly one half of his war budget came from Swiss bankers.

Geneva was a very prosperous city in the seventeenth century due to its advantageous trade position. Many of her citizens were happy to invest in French bonds that would provide a return on their savings. Suddenly, however, with France's defeat in 1713 many of the war debts went bad and Geneva was thrown into a

Berne. View of the Old Town and the Houses of Parliament.

recession. A large number of "bankers," that is, those who had acted as financial intermediaries during the war, now had to declare bankruptcy.

Geneva, though, was able to survive the crisis quite well. Thanks to the large number of successful trading and financial firms the economy proved resilient enough to weather the default of the French bonds. To avoid a recurrence of such problems the Geneva City Council produced a series of civil edicts aimed at reforming local commerce and regulating the activities of investment brokers. The aim of these edicts was to encourage sound investment and money lending practices and to promote the maintenance of free enterprise.

An interesting offshoot of these edicts was a statute which established the right of financial clients to confidential treatment:

> The [brokers] shall keep accurate records of all their dealings for the purpose of reference and shall not furnish extracts thereof, unless by order of the council, to any person other than those on whose behalf they have acted.

As early as the eighteenth century, then, respect for personal freedom had led to the codification of "banking" secrecy in Switzerland. Nearly two centuries later this concept of banking secrecy would become a political rallying cry for the Swiss and an anathema to repressive foreign governments.

There was also a rallying cry of another sort in the late 18th century and that was the political gospel of Jean Jacques Rousseau, who was born in Geneva in 1712. His ideas would restructure the political organization of much of Europe, Switzerland included. To the Swiss Rousseau's doctrine of sovereignty for the people was very compatible with the old ideals of Swiss confederation. Yet, the revolutionary fervor that was felt in France was missing in Switzerland. The Swiss, though generally favouring the ideals of a republic, were much too traditionalist and distrustful of a new social order to give it a go.

Their patriotic neighbors, the French, however, would not take no for an answer and overran Switzerland. For the first time the confederation failed as the cantons could not agree to bind together against the French attack. The Swiss had ambiguous feelings about a new government.

In 1798 the French gave the Swiss a new constitution and

Geneva. The bronze statue of the world famous philosopher and poet Jean-Jacques Rousseau (1712-78).

created a new republic, "The Helvetic Republic." The response of the Swiss was indifferent, to say the least. Administratively, though, the occupation was a boon to Switzerland. What was left of the aristocracy lost their privileges, and trade grew more rapidly amongst the cantons as barriers, both political and economic, diminished under the new regime. Still, the new republic, no matter how democratic it professed to be, could not offer the liberty and democratic rights enjoyed by the Swiss before the French invasion. People were still loyal to their cantons and any infringement upon cantonal rights to self—determination was taken as an infringement upon their personal rights. Several cantons rebelled, but without success. The political climate in Switzerland continued to show that it did not lend itself to centralized government.

Relief came to Switzerland with the defeat of Napoleon in 1813. In the wake of the Napoleonic Empire the map of Europe was redrawn. At the Congress of Vienna in 1815 Switzerland's borders, as they exist today, were determined. More important-ly, it was also decided to recognize Swiss neutrality in internation-al law and a declaration was issued guaranteeing the integrity and inviolability of Swiss territory.

Swiss neutrality was by no means an act of charity by the great powers, as they themselves stated in the treaty: "The neutrality and integrity of Switzerland and its independence from any foreign influence are in the true interests of all European states." Swiss neutrality, in effect, gave the rest of Europe a buffer zone.

In order for the Swiss to maintain their neutrality they would have to take a very active role in preserving it. In the nearly two centuries since the Congress of Vienna the wariness, tradition-alism and multi—lingual character of the Swiss have aided them in the maintenance of a cautious policy of neutrality.

It would take the Swiss the rest of the 19th century to consolidate their position after the Congress of Vienna. The 19th century was a time of reaction and regeneration for the Swiss. Many reforms were brought through during the quarter century after 1815. In general the sovereignty of the people was increased during this time. Government was made more representative. The cities became less powerful. Censorship was abolished and freedom of press and speech encouraged. From all over Europe refugees came into Switzerland. Switzerland was a melting pot for political idealists both right and left.

Reconciliation between the cantons was a major theme in politics when the constitution of 1848 was written. A small revolution the year before had made all the Swiss aware of the fact that if the people of Switzerland were to have their sovereignty, then the cantons of Switzerland would have to relinquish some of theirs. The Constitution was written to be very flexible and it has survived until today because of its malleability and because the cantons have been willing to compromise their sovereignty in order to participate more fully in Swiss confederation.

The Switzerland which faced the 20th century was not a strong country but it was adaptable; its people were not totally satisfied, but they were politically experienced and if there was a lack of nationalistic spirit, there was a strong will to survive. The power struggles of the 20th century would harden the political acumen of the Swiss and make them more confident of their ability to survive.

The Swiss banking industry, meanwhile, was also finding it had to be very flexible in order to meet the needs of the rapidly growing economy. As the twentieth century drew closer the Swiss banking system was about to take a central role in Swiss society.

In 1862 there were some twenty registered banks in Switzerland. All were rather small. They were not in the business of issuing notes but did collect bills of exchange for account and made payments of checks and drafts against credit. They were 'private' banks, that is, privately run and owned by a small group of individuals. To remain competitive in the domestic banking industry many of the private bankers realized they would have to form syndicates to take advantage of the economics of scale. By joining together, the banks found it much easier to become involved in larger transactions as they were able to spread the risk out among their members. One of these syndicates formed from the firms of Bischoff, Ehinger, Merian, Passavant, Riggenbach and Sneyer took the name Bank-Verein (Bank Corporation). Today the Swiss Bank Corporation, with its headquarters in Basel, is the largest bank in Switzerland.

Such syndicates along with their counterparts elsewhere in Switzerland did a lot to finance the industrial revolution in France. These banks had attracted large sums of money from the Swiss and Germans and were now looking for ways to invest this capital. By financing the growing industries in France they were able to realize such an opportunity. Switzerland was able to provide France with the funds to mechanize wool and silk production, and to develop and expand her metallurgical industries.

Zürich began to function as a banking center at about this time. Prior to the nineteenth century manufacturers in Zürich had had little need for private bankers as they were quite capable of financing themselves. After the Swiss Confederation was formed in 1848 and a standard currency was created, Switzerland moved rapidly to modernize and integrate its economy. The creation of a rail system linking the major Swiss cities to each other and to their neighboring countries was an important step towards the completion of these goals.

Alfred Escher, a merchant and former mayor of Zürich, pushed Zürich to the foreground as a financial center by creating the Schweizerische Kreditanstalt (Swiss Credit Bank) which would, along with similar credit institutions, finance a large part of the development of Swiss industry and the construction of Switzerland's major rail lines. Before Escher had organized the Kreditanstalt (1856) there were only two banks in Zürich and neither one was in the business of large scale lending. Escher solved this problem by molding the Schweizerische Kreditanstalt after the French Crédit Mobilier. The charter he drew up for his bank expressly followed the form of the French Crédit Mobilier. The Swiss Credit Bank (Kreditanstalt) was allowed to grant loans or credits, participate in both new and old enterprises, issue securities and its own bonds, discount bills, buy and sell precious metals, stocks or merchandise and accept deposits.[2] This then was a bank in the modern sense; no longer just a depository or trading house for gold and silver coin.

When it came time to raise equity capital for the Swiss Credit Bank, a German firm, the Allgemeine Deutsche Kreditanstalt of Leipzig was willing to contribute 50% of the capital needed.

Escher and his associates, although willing to take the money, clearly stipulated that control of the Bank must always remain in Swiss hands. They did not want any outside interests to get a chance at controlling Swiss industries. The Allgemeine Deutsche Kreditanstalt agreed to subscribe 7.5 million Swiss francs without seeking any control of the bank. Escher and his co—founders subscribed to another 3 million and the balance of 3 million Swiss francs was offered to the public. The public was given the chance to purchase 6,000 shares of stock. Within three days Escher had orders for 436,539 shares at a par value of over 218 million francs. Banking got off to a booming start in Zürich and, with the public's confidence obviously behind it, was destined to continue growing right up to the present.

The Swiss Credit Bank and others like it prospered in a very short time. Money that was brought out of hiding was now being put to good use. In Basel, Geneva and Zürich banks sprung up to accept peoples' savings and make investments in such large scale projects as the Goddard Tunnel and the Swiss rail lines. The connection between Swiss banking and Swiss industrialization was being forged. The two grew hand in hand. Rapid industrialization meant growth for the Swiss banking system. Banks began to issue overdrafts and unsecured loans to further develop their domestic markets. Local cantonal banks, to meet the needs of local commerce, would have to attract capital from outside their borders. Bank directors became deeply involved in insurance, railroads, electrical works, factories and exports. The Swiss public became more conscious of the role banking could play in the expansion of the Swiss economy.

By the end of the nineteenth century industrialization was so successful and the economic strength of Switzerland was such that Swiss banks could once again export capital, that is to say, provide loans and make investments abroad. During this era, for example, we can find Swiss banks making loans to the Danish, Russian and Roumanian governments, as well as investing in the preferred stock and bonds of many American corporations.[3] Many Swiss industrial and insurance companies began setting up affiliated companies abroad. The days of industrialization were days of financial integration both domestically, as banks found themselves coming together to float big loans, and internationally,

Geneva's famous jet d'eau vives, reaching a height of 140 meters.

as banks and other corporations moved beyond the borders of Switzerland in search of new markets.

With the advent of World War I came an abrupt end to this rapid development as trade and financial relations were disrupted. Banks that had invested abroad were hard hit. Swiss assets abroad shrank from 8 to 2.5 million Swiss francs as the German and Austrian currencies collapsed. Switzerland, although neutral, was in the unenviable position of having to depend on the belligerent nations for her imports. Yet, the strain on her economy was far less than that suffered by the other European nations.

By 1920, in the aftermath of the war, nearly every European country had put restrictions on foreign loans and investments. They thought that by keeping their money at home they could more quickly rebuild their countries. This was a very short sighted policy; what was the use of forcing capital markets into relative isolation in a world that was clearly economically interdependent. The result was that little real growth could be produced. The economies of the major European countries were in a shambles and demands for reparations from Germany, coupled with capital restrictions, doomed them to more serious trouble.

In Switzerland, however, there were no foreign exchange restrictions and the Swiss franc, thanks to Switzerland's political neutrality and economic stability, remained literally as good as gold. The condition of the Swiss economy remained quite serene when compared to the tumultuous economic upheaval suffered in the rest of Europe. Before World War I the banking industry in Switzerland followed a course of development that was similar to that experienced by its European neighbors. Conditions after World War I marked a turning point for the Swiss banking industry as it set off on a course of development all its own. Switzerland found that its role as an international banking and financial center was not limited solely to providing loans and investments for the rest of Europe.

Switzerland also became important as a safe depository for foreign funds. The Swiss franc was stable, the government respected private property and the economy flourished under free enterprise. Swiss banks became a haven for foreign funds that were threatened by inflation and political instability at home.

Money flowed into Switzerland and the Swiss bankers were quick to service their new clients and help them get their money into Switzerland.

During the depression foreign capital again sought refuge in Switzerland because the risk of devaluation there was least. Switzerland, as a result, managed to come through the depression quite well as compared to other Western countries. With money coming in from abroad Swiss industry was able to borrow at lower rates domestically.

World War II again prompted frightened people to send their money and properties to Switzerland for safekeeping. German businessmen who wanted to keep their businesses out of Nazi control tried to have ownership of their firms transferred to a Swiss corporation. Although this was possible, it was often a very dangerous transaction as it was strictly prohibited by the Nazi government. Offenders were severely punished and often even killed for treason. Nevertheless Swiss banks continued to receive considerable sums of money from Germany, particularly from the Jews.

To thwart the inquisitiveness of the Gestapo the Swiss made it a criminal offense, in the banking code of 1934, for foreign agents to elicit information about bank accounts. Furthermore, bankers themselves were not allowed, under this new penal code, to provide any information regarding the existence of an account to any outsiders. Switzerland served notice on the world that it would protect its foreign deposits and insure that banking clients would receive the discretion they wanted.

The maintenance of this banking code caused problems for the Swiss not only during the War but also in the immediate post-War period. The Americans, for example, were certain that Swiss banks were holding large amounts of German assets in trusts which they wanted liquidated and used for war reparations. the Swiss, who had defended many German holdings against Nazi pressures, now found themselves fighting American demands which threatened to compromise their neutrality. The Americans were, at first, quite adamant in their claims. They even went so far as to decree that an allied Commission be set up in Switzerland to supervise the seizure and liquidation of German assets.

Admittedly, among the German assets transferred to Switzerland were some large holdings of what were Nazi controlled firms during the War. A particular example is the famous case of the I.G. Farben-International chemical conglomerate. The Swiss, though agreeable to allowing the confiscation of any assets that were clearly Nazi procured, were hesitant to allow the confiscation of any private property. Tradition, law, and especially practical experience, had taught the Swiss the importance of applying their neutrality unilaterally. If Swiss neutrality is to survive it must be applicable and in force at all times and under all circumstances.

In the end, though, the Swiss found it difficult to stand up against the power of the United States in post-War Europe. Both parties got together to negotiate a compromise in which the Americans relieved some of their economic and political pressures in return for the Swiss liquidating several German firms. The money obtained from these liquidations was used for war reparations. Through the late 40's and early 50's cooperation between the Swiss and Americans in promoting the recovery of Europe grew steadily. Finally in 1952 the matter of liquidating German firms was settled; with the Swiss government agreeing to indemnify German citizens for all the private assets of businesses given up to the Allies.[4]

In retrospect, we can say that Swiss banks were only slightly scarred by World War II. There were several banks that were forced into receivership but, in general, the image of Swiss bankers improved rather than diminished. They demonstrated in their stand, first against the Nazis, and then against the Americans, that they had great regard for their foreign depositors, whomever they might be. Internationally, Switzerland had asserted her role as a haven for foreign capital.

Politically, by surviving both the World Wars as a neutral bystander, Switzerland was able to gain the respect of the whole world. Practically, too, it had provided an example for all small independent states and proven that non-alignment was possible. Switzerland remained neutral for many reasons: there was political determination, there was economic necessity and there was a responsibility to all those who had trusted in Switzerland. There was also the fact that Switzerland is a land of many cultures, a country with a unique ability to appreciate both sides of an issue and thereby be better able to come to terms with it. When it was all over the Swiss were imbued with a sense of nationalism.

In the immediate post-War period the Swiss banks began to export capital again, especially to those countries that needed to rebuild after the War.

Many foreign firms also moved into Switzerland to do business. Foreign banks and multinational corporations established demand and time deposits with Swiss banks. As there was no domestic money market of adequate absorbing capacity, the banks reinvested these funds abroad. The interdependence between the Swiss banking system and foreign economies increased rapidly. By combining banking know-how with a unique economic climate Switzerland achieved status as an international financial center.

Politically and economically the Swiss were able to mature to the point where they represented an alternative to those who needed it.

For centuries, the Swiss had been forced to seek abroad what they could not find at home. Determined to keep their independence, but lacking the needed natural resources, the Swiss were thrown into economic assimilation with their neighbors.

Whether by fighting abroad as soldiers, granting credit to finance other economies or trading, Swiss economic development was achieved by having the Swiss move their business into the outside world. Through the sale and exchange of goods and services in those early days, the Swiss laid the foundations for their present day network of business and banking interests abroad.

After Switzerland had developed into a modern industrial state the banks in Switzerland found themselves with sufficient liquidity to lend abroad. Capital export grew not only out of the fact that there were too few investments opportunities at home but also because Switzerland was dependent on the economies of her neighbors and had an interest, therefore, in their well-being.

Through diversification and internationalization the banking system of Switzerland had outgrown the bounds of its country. Particularly, within the last two decades the Swiss banking

Tour Baudet (15th Century) in Geneva, now the Town Hall.

system had expanded at a phenomenal rate. Today banking may well be the most important industry in Switzerland. As of the end of 1978 there were 469 banks with nearly 80,000 employees and 4,800 branches for a population of 6.3 million Swiss.

PART II

THE SWISS
BANKING SYSTEM

The Swiss Banking Structure

The Swiss banking system has been divided into several distinct classifications by the statisticians at the Swiss National Bank. These classifications exist, in part, because of the historical role each type of bank has played in the development of the Swiss economy. In recent years with the growing internationalization of the Swiss banking industry the divisions between the role and duties of each type of bank have become less clear and it is expected that this trend will continue.

CHAPTER ONE

The Big Banks

Historically this classification was made up of those banks which were largest in terms of overall business. Except for the first three of this group however, this is no longer true.

All of these banks cover the whole range of banking and investment activities for their clients. Unlike banks in the United States they are not limited in their activities by the Glass Steagall Act. Banks in Switzerland can be both commercial and investment banks at the same time. Though universal banks predominate in Switzerland, it is mostly the "big banks" that truly engage in universal banking activities. They handle foreign exchange transactions, savings and loans, commercial financing and act as brokers for precious metals and securities worldwide. The Union Bank of Switzerland (Schweizerische Bankgesellschaft), the Swiss Bank Corporation (Schweizerische Bankverein), and the Swiss Credit Bank (Schweizerische Kreditanstalt) stand head and shoulders above all other Swiss banks and are heavily involved in international dealings with branch offices around the world.

When compared with other banks in the world by the size of their balance sheets the two largest Swiss banks find themselves in about the fiftieth position. The reader should remember however that the balance sheets of Swiss banks only tell part of the story. The numbers published by the banks in their balance sheets do not include a) the sums of money they manage for clients as brokers, or b) their fiduciary accounts. It is important also to take into consideration both of these sums when attempting to evaluate the impact of Swiss banks on the international economic scene.

The fiduciary accounts held by the bank represent a wide range of investments including precious metals, securities, and

TABLE 1

The Big Banks

Year Founded	Head Office	Bank	Total Assets*
1872	Basel	Schweizerischer Bankverein	65,246,900
1912	Zürich	Schweizerische Bankgesellschaft	65,431,200
1856	Zürich	Schweizerische Kreditanstalt	52,814,500
1896	Bern	Schweizerische Volksbank	14,793,700
1755	Zurich	Bank Leu	4,645,400

*in thousands of Swiss francs—from estimates made by the Swiss National Bank for September 1979.

certificates of deposit. All fiduciary accounts are held in the bank's name for the client. Technically the Swiss bank is not to be held liable for the performance of these accounts. The account holder must agree to hold such an account at the bank solely at his own risk. To give an idea of the size of these fiduciary accounts the Swiss National Bank has estimated that the total of fiduciary credits controlled by Swiss banks as of the beginning of 1980 was approximately 57 billion Swiss francs, and this is most certainly an understatement.

Swiss banks also control vast sums through the management of their clients' assets. The size of the portfolios which Swiss banks manage is unknown as it does not appear on their balance sheet. Although it may be impossible to estimate just how much Swiss banks control through such money management, it would not be too presumptuous to guess that on the average Swiss banks manage twice again what appear as assets on their balance sheets.

The importance of the "big banks" is also to be felt in other ways. They are all, along with the Groupement des Banquier Privés Génévois and the Cantonal Bank of Bern, members of the influential Cartel of Swiss Banks which handles the underwriting and the bond issues of the Treasury. Additionally these banks handle the largest part of the business in the Swiss stock exchanges. Most of the smaller banks do their security trading and account clearing through one or more of the "big banks." They are also the leading dealers in the foreign exchange market (this applies to the three largest of the "big banks"). The volume of foreign exchange transactions carried on by these "big banks" is on the order of three billion dollars a day. It is no wonder that they are so often said to be responsible for exchange rate fluctuations.

As of the end of 1979 the "big banks" were accountable for 48% of the total credit granted by the Swiss banks. These credits, granted both domestically and abroad, were for industry, constuction trade and commerce. Also included are mortgage credits for which the "big banks" loaned out 33% of the total. Kleincredit (medium term cash loan) is also granted by three of the "big banks" and they account for 15% of the credit granted in this category.

The five "big banks" held a total of 8.32 billion Swiss francs in securities on their balance sheets as of the end of 1978. This represented just over 4% of their combined total balance. Of this amount 14% were bonds and stocks of Swiss banks, 19% were bonds and stocks of Swiss industry and finance companies, 17% were government bonds, 10% were bonds of the canton and community, and 40% came from foreign stocks and bonds. It is interesting to note here the increased investment by the "big banks" in foreign stocks and bonds. Only ten years ago the percentage of foreign securities held by the "big banks" was only 15% of the total amount of securities they had.

Swiss banks under Section III, Article 4 of the Swiss Federal Banking Law are required to keep an adequate relation between: "a) their own resources and their total liabilities; b) their liquid assets and their marketable assets on one side and their short-term liabilities on the other side." Banks must periodically file liquidity statements (see Appendix I) and meet the liquidity and reserve requirements as stipulated in Section V of the Implementing Ordinance for the Federal Banking Law (May 1972).

The Swiss Banking Commission reserves the right to change the provisions for these requirements when they see fit. The formula by which liquidity requirements are calculatd is quite complex and, for practical purposes, beyond the scope of this paper. The liquidity calculation statement in the Appendix can give the reader an idea of how the banks are to calculate their positions. According to the latest statistics of the Swiss National

Bank there are two grades of liquidity that a bank meets (see Appendix II). In general when using such criteria Swiss banks are found to be much more liquid than their United States counter-parts.

All of the "big banks" are publicly owned and their shares traded on the Zürich Stock Exchange. Their net profits (published) amounted to about 850 million Swiss francs in 1978. Over two-thirds of these earnings came from their foreign businesses. As universal banks they have literally outgrown their domestic banking function. It is estimated that somewhat over one-half of their balance sheet is composed of foreign assets.

CHAPTER 2

Cantonal Banks

Legally the cantonal banks are state banks, created not by the Federal authorities but rather by the individual states (cantons) in Switzerland. Switzerland's 25 cantons have a total of 28 cantonal banks, as Berne, Geneva and Vaud each have two cantonal banks. Of these 28 institutions, 23 are furnished with both state capital and with state guarantees. The other five, the cantonal banks of Zug, Vaud and Geneva, each have either a state guarantee or state capital, but not both. In terms of total assets the cantonal banks rank second in importance behind the "big banks" with over 88 billion Swiss francs in assets on their combined balance sheets. The size of cantonal banks varies greatly from canton to canton. The largest, the Zürcher Cantonalbank has a balance sheet total of more than 16 billion Swiss francs. This makes it the fourth largest bank in Switzerland in terms of total assets, just behind the "big three." Most of the other cantonal banks have balance sheet totals of between 1 and 5 billion Swiss francs.

Historically, the demand for public financial institutions like the cantonal bank goes back a long way. Their original purpose was to support and supplement the activity of privately owned banks within their respective cantons. With the beginning of industrialization and the growth of free trade and commerce it became increasingly difficult for those in agriculture and small businesses to find credit. The private bankers during the boom years withdrew their loans from mortgages to turn to more profitable investments in industry and export trade. Many cantonal banks were set up to fill this void; today they still satisfy the credit needs of the private householder, the craftsman and the merchant with the most favorable possible terms. In 1979, for example, the average interest rate for mortgage investments was 4.11% at the cantonal banks or about .05-.1% better than at the "big banks." This in part explains why the cantonal banks control nearly 45% of all mortgages placed with Swiss banks.

They are able to maintain these lower mortgage rates largely as a result of their structure and the importance of their state guarantee. With the cantonal government standing behind the bank, people feel more secure about depositing their savings at a cantonal bank. Furthermore, the cantonal banks are all known for the conservative nature of their investments. These factors combined make the cantonal banks the safest possible place for public money and because of this they are normally able to offer a lower interest rate than other banks. As of the end of 1978, they were as a rule paying 2 to 2 1/4% on savings accounts while other banks paid 2 1/4 to 2 1/2%. Despite this difference in rates the cantonal banks are still able to offer an attractive investment for people's savings. Their success in this regard is illustrated by the fact that in 1978 40% of all the savings held in Swiss banks was being held by cantonal banks.

Although for several decades the cantonal banks dealt chiefly with pure mortgage transactions this situation has changed considerably in recent years. Due to the growing economy and competition from other banks, the cantonal banks have been developing themselves into full service banks. Today's cantonal bank is usually quite involved in commercial loans and the purchase and sale of stocks and bonds. They play an important role in arranging capital issues, especially for the state and municipalities. Not only are they of primary imporance in raising capital for these local governments but, as of 1972, they were also admitted en bloc into the Cartel of Swiss Banks for foreign bond issues.

Nevertheless, despite their growth and diversification the cantonal banks still are basically regional banks. The foreign loans of these banks amount to about 1% of their total assets. Generally foreign investments and loans by cantonal banks are prohibited by law. This may soon be changing however, as some of the cantonal banks, like the "big banks" before them, are outgrowing the investment opportunities of their territorial boundaries. The larger cantonal banks manage to get around this by investing abroad indirectly. By underwriting foreign bonds, for example, they become indirectly involved in the foreign market. Also when they invest their surplus funds with the "big banks", the "big banks" in turn will most likely use these funds in their international transactions. To change the laws which prohibit cantonal banks from engaging in foreign business will require a national referendum. The cantonal banks are confident that this will be coming soon and the law will be changed.

The 28 Swiss cantonal banks, to look after their common interests, joined together in 1907 to form the Association of Cantonal Banks. This Association functions to promote the business and protect the integrity of the cantonal banks in a number of ways. First of all, the Association represents the interests of its members to the Federal authorities, for example, in the drafting and implementation of banking laws applicable to the cantonal banks. Secondly, the Association coordinates activities between the cantonal banks, such as advertising, adopting a uniform accounting system, and account clearing among the banks. Finally, the Association supervises the issuance of state and municipal bonds, the management of intra bank funds, and the regulation of mortgage interest rates.

The cantonal banks are the backbone of domestic banking in Switzerland. They have continually grown to meet the needs of their respective cantons and seem assured of being able to continue to do so in the future.

CHAPTER 3

Regional and Savings Banks

Regional and Savings Banks, like the cantonal banks, specialize in domestic business. They were originally formed to meet the needs of the rising middle classes in Switzerland during the 19th century. Most of them are joint stock undertakings or cooperatives that were organized to collect savings and then meet the financial requirements of their shareholders who were usually employed in small businesses or agriculture. It is, nowadays, difficult to differentiate within this statistical category between savings banks, mortgage banks, and commercial banks working on a regional level. The structural differences between these banks have become quite small over the years.

The savings banks are probably the easiest to set apart in this category. They are unique in that they invest their money only to the extent necessary to pay interest on their savings deposits and to clear their overhead. They are not out to earn big profits but rather to provide the community with an incentive to save. The savings bank business, however, is not restricted solely to savings banks. According to Article 15 of the Federal Banking Law savings deposits may be accepted by all banks that publish an annual statement of condition. There are presently just over 80 savings banks and some 250 banks altogether, that accept savings accounts. At the end of 1978, of a total of 88 billion Swiss francs in savings accounts, 20.1 billion (23%) was held by regional and savings banks.

Another interesting characteristic of savings banks in Switzerland is that there is no federal law controlling the investment activities of these banks. They are not at all restricted in the types of investments they made. Under the Federal Banking Law, however, savings accounts under 5,000 Swiss francs are privileged in the case of bankruptcy (Article 15). Article 16 of the

Banking Law further authorizes the cantons "to create a statutory lien not exceeding 5,000 francs on the securities and claims of such (savings) banking offices."

Despite what might seem to be a lot of competition from other commercial banks and financial intermediaries the savings banks still seem to be faring quite well. However, they are growing at a slower rate than the other banks in Switzerland.

The regional and mortgage banks differ from the savings banks somewhat in their legal status. In the case of the mortgage banks the assets are made up of at least 60% mortgage loans. The means by which these mortgage banks obtain long term credit are chiefly through two channels: one is long term deposit and investment savings accounts and the other is the issuance of cash obligations (interest bearing certificates of deposit, 3-8 years). For the most part these mortgage banks, with the exception of three or four large ones, restrict their banking activities to this immediate area. In a country which has the highest per capita rate of mortgages, the mortgage banks are certain to remain an integral part of the financial system.

The other local banks that, along with the mortgage banks, make up the classification regional banks are generally banks engaged mainly in local commercial business. Banks in this category, which are neither strictly savings nor mortgage banks, are sometimes designated "middlebanks." They are somewhere between the specialized savings and mortgage banks and the full service banks of the big cities. This group of banks has been facing difficulties in recent years due to the changing structure of the Swiss economy. As local industries become export-oriented, these banks find that they are too small, lacking sufficient know-how and capital to service their clients properly. Modern technology has made banking much more competitive than it used to be, and the smaller institutions will either have to attract business by specialization or face the danger of being out-competed. In many cases these smaller banks are simply taken over by the cantonal bank or one of the "big three banks."

CHAPTER 4

Loan Associations

The 1204 credit cooperatives in Switzerland have assets equal to 2.9% of total Swiss banking assets. They are grouped into two associations: the largest one, the Schweizer Verband der Raiffeisenkassen, as 1190 affiliated cooperatives and a total balance of 11.1 billion Swiss francs; the other, the Federation Vandoise des Caisses de Credit Mutuel, has 14 affiliated cooperatives and a balance of 82 million Swiss francs. The total assets of the Schweizer Verband der Raiffeisenkassen is quite large when compared with other Swiss banks. In fact, when comparing combined assets, it is bigger than one of the "big five banks" and all but one of the cantonal banks.

The Raiffeisen banks are named after F. W. Raiffeisen, who was, back in 1848, the mayor of a group of villages around Neuwied in Germany. Determined to alleviate the economic distress his district was suffering from, Raiffeisen saw that the only means for improvement lay with the people themselves. The function of his Raiffeisen associations was "to improve the situation of its members ... to obtain through a common guarantee the necessary capital for granting loans to members for the development of their business and their household, and to bring idle capital into productive use". Any earnings which may which may come out of such a bank are to be returned to benefit the which may come out of such a bank are to be returned to benefit the community from which they accumulated.[1]

These Raiffeisen banks are usually set up in agricultural communities which are too small to have a bank of their own. Anyone within the particular community may make a deposit into the Raiffeisen bank but only those who are members may apply for a loan. The interest rates payable on the deposits are comparable to those offered by other savings banks in the country. Loans granted to members of the association must be secured. Acceptable forms of collateral are marketable securities, third party guarantees, and mortgages on dwellings and private property. (Loans to public bodies and joint liability cooperatives are an exception and require no collateral). It must be realized that the risk involved in all such loans is quite low. Since the Raiffeisen associations are always limited to a small community the people who take out loans are always well known to the members of the association. Even if the borrower has good collateral he must also be known in his private life to be of good standing if he is to receive a loan. Additionally, the association requires to know not only the character of the borrower, but also the specific object for which the loan is intended. The association must be satisfied the borrower will employ the loan for a useful purpose and that the operation proposed is likely to turn out successfully.

The interest rates on the loans granted are always kept at the lowest possible level. The loan associations are able to actively compete in the money market because of their low overhead. No paid staff members are really required and a respected citizen in the community usually has the responsibility of handling the books.

Since their inception the loan associations have been an impetus in the Swiss economy. Although the Swiss economy is no longer heavily agricultural the loan association continues to serve the 'agricultural' communities. The growing number of small businesses continues to find financing from loan associations attractive. The following chart shows how they have been steadily growing in number over the years. (See chart, p. 41)

The loan associations which are part of the Raiffeissen System have a central bank for all their activities. Die Zentralbank des Schweizer Verbandes der Raiffeisenkassen. This central bank is the clearing center for all the associated Raiffeissen banks. The central bank also plays an important role as a supervisory authority. They supervise audits and centralize the bookkeeping operations of the 1183 Raiffeissen banks.

The loan associations in Switzerland have been successful in providing credit to the rural districts. Whereas they were originally organized to provide credit for the small agriculturalist, they now are an important source of credit for the rural businessman. The flexibility of these loan associations has made them one of the fastest growing institutions in the Swiss financial sector. By channeling what would otherwise have been unproductive capital into productive use, these institutions have been largely responsible for the success of economic development on the local level.

TABLE 2

Year	Number of Loan Associations	Total Assets (Million Francs)
1903	25	1.76
1923	332	136
1945	753	599
1955	1020	1404
1962	1101	2439
1967	1127	3684
1970	1142	4820
1973	1174	7046
1976	1192	9416
1979	1204	11191

CHAPTER 5

Private Banks

It is probably the private Swiss banks that have done the most to perpetuate the mystique of Swiss banking. The uniqueness of the private bank in Switzerland comes from the discretionary air with which they conduct their business. If you were to visit one of these banks, say, for example, Vontobel & Cie in Zurich you would find a bronze plaque on street level and offices, perhaps, on the third floor. Advertising is practically non-existent, and from their outward appearance these banks seem anything but the successful traditional banking houses that they are.

By law the 27 private banks in Switzerland are not required to publish their balance sheets. It is estimated that each of the major private banks has assets of between 200 and 600 million Swiss francs. The real importance of the private banks lies with the amount of funds that they manage. The larger private banks manage portfolios of between six and eight billion Swiss francs each, as estimated by Hans Bär, partner J. Bär & Co. (formerly a private bank). For nearly a century most of these private banks have been catering to a select and wealthy clientele as investment counsellors and financial managers.

The private banks are very actively involved in the area of securities trading. They trade heavily not only on the Swiss exchanges but also on all other major exchanges abroad. Their holdings are widely diversified throughout the world. In Zürich the Groupement de Banquiers Privée Zürichois was formed in 1962 from the private banks: Julius Bär & Cie (since that time this bank, once the largest private bank, has now become incorporated), Rahn und Badmer, Rud Blass & Cie, J. Vontobel, and Wegelin and Cie. This group was formed to be competitive with the"big banks"in the underwriting of foreign bond issues in Swiss francs and other currencies. There is also a similar group, the Groupement Genèvois, in Geneva, also composed of private banks, that was founded to engage in the same business. Private banks now control about 3% of the Swiss franc foreign bond issues.

The management of the private banks is almost always held by the general partners who, in most cases, have inherited control of the bank. An important characteristic of private banking is that the partners have unlimited liability to their clients. There are advantages and disadvantages to this situation. From the clients' perspective unlimited liability of the partners means that the banks are more likely to be cautious with their funds. Private banks, in fact, are considerably more cautious about their investments than, for example, an average commercial bank. Private banks are also renowned for the personal way in which they conduct business. The partners often know all their clients personally and are in frequent contact with them. This is understandable when one remembers that many private banks will not handle accounts of less than $50,000 to $100,000.

From the banker's perspective, however, private control without incorporation can be quite a headache. There are many tax problems and, of course, the threat of having your personal fortune liquidated in bad times. Additionally, there are the problems of finding an able successor and avoiding the pitfalls of stagnating management. As the private banks become increasingly competitive and expansionary there will be increasing pressure on the partners to incorporate. In fact, since the end of World War II, the number of private banks has declined from 83 to 27 as this trend has been gathering momentum.

The forte of the private banks, as already mentioned, is to be found in their small, select number of clients and their diversified personal service. They are ideally suited to administer the private property of their clients. Managing portfolios, establishing trusts, and advising on international investments are the primary means by which the private banks earn their profits. The typical private bank in Switzerland has an international outlook. It controls vast amounts of foreign assets which we can only guess at.

Although there is little information made public on the condition or size of the private banks they are still quite carefully regulated. The Swiss National Bank requires a monthly balance sheet from each of the private banks. All the banks subject themselves to standard external audits and the larger private banks have their own internal auditing departments. Nevertheless, as one private banker told me, "There still are accidents." For example, Leclerc & Cie, founded in Geneva in 1856, is now in receivership as a result of speculative real estate holdings it had in Germany during the 60's. Since private banks never issue financial statements one would think that an event like this might tarnish their respectability but that is not the case. They continue to be revered and trusted not only by foreigners but also by other bankers in Switzerland.

The private bankers in Switzerland play an important role in attracting funds from abroad. They cater to a select and diverse group of international investors and although they provide the service of a small bank they are sufficiently sophisticated to handle all sorts of international dealings for their clients. The personality of the Swiss private banking firm may have been formed in the 19th century but their character is very much a part of the 20th century.

CHAPTER 6

Other Swiss Banks

Under the classification of "other banks" the Swiss National Bank distinguishes between those "other banks" which are Swiss held (98) and those that are owned by foreigners (85). The banks in this miscellaneous grouping operate, for the most part, as innovators in expanding specialized sectors of banking. We find in this category, therefore, installment credit institutions, banks specializing in foreign trade financing, stock exchange and security transactions, and trust administration. Many of the banks in this category of "other banks" function just as the private banks do. They are, however, incorporated and the shareholders do not have unlimited personal liability for the liabilities of the bank. Like the private banks the "other banks" in general thrive on their international business. As of the beginning of 1978 the foreign operations of "other banks" accounted for about 60% of their assets and 45% of their liabilities. They accounted for 22% of all foreign lending and 30% of all foreign deposits held in Switzerland.

The foreign controlled banks in Switzerland have grown tremendously in importance over the past quarter century. As the world became heavily financially interdependent in the post World War II era major banks abroad were quick to establish branch offices in Switzerland. Nearly all the major American, French, Italian and Japanese banks have banks in Switzerland too. The impact of these foreign controlled banks on the Swiss banking industry has been quite extensive. They offer considerable competition to the domestic banks not only in terms of offering their services to multinational companies but also in competing with local banks for managerial staff. Making use of their international connections, these foreign banks take advantage of the economies of scale and have been doing quite a successful business in Switzerland.

The Palais des Nations in Geneva, the European seat of the United Nations.

CHAPTER 7

Mortgage Bonds and Mortgage Institutions

These Mortgage Bond Banks (Pfandbriefzentralen) were created by "Issue of Mortgage Bonds Act" of June 1930 to provide banks engaged in the mortgage business with long term funds on relatively favorable terms. During the Depression many banks learned the hard way the difficulties of holding short term bonds and savings to finance long term mortgage. The Mortgage Bond Banks were created to give these banks an opportunity to convert their short term bonds into longer term mortgage bonds. Many mortgage banks, especially the smaller ones were able to acquire long term funds at relatively favorable rates and thus improve the structure of their financial holdings. A result of this was a greater stabilization of interest rates for mortgages.

The Mortgage Bond Banks are limited by law to the issue of mortgage bonds with a maturity of between 15 and 40 years; the funds thus acquired may be loaned only to member banks against the security of mortgages entered in the mortgage register. The volume of the banks lending is limited to twenty times its paid in capital. Both of these banks are subject to the Federal Banking Law. The mortgage bonds issued by these banks are quoted on the major Swiss stock exchanges. This assures bond holders of good marketability for their mortgage bond assets.

Whereas each of the 28 cantonal banks is a member of the Central Mortgage Bond Office of the cantonal banks, only those banks with 60% of their assets consisting of mortgage loans have a legal right to participate in the Mortgage Bond Bank of Swiss Mortgage Institutions. The amount of loans granted by these banks is 4.3 billion Swiss francs and 3.8 billion (December, 1977) respectively. This in total represents nearly 8% of all mortgages outstanding in Switzerland.

CHAPTER 8

Other Financial Institutions

Investment trusts

The investment trusts, or mutual funds as they are known to Americans exhibited quite rapid growth in the 60s but as of late their growth rates are down drastically as investments in securities and real estate have been depreciating. A number of banks have begun their own investment trusts in order to provide the small investor with a means to take advantage of a bank's portfolio management services.

According to law an investment trust may only invest its assets in marketable securities or real estate. The by-laws of the trust must be approved by the Federal Banking Commission. The investment trust as well as the managing company are required to undergo periodic examination by independent auditors. They must publish a report on their activities yearly and satisfy their legal requirements as set for by the Federal Act on Mutual funds of July 1966. Included in these requirements to protect investors is the stipulation that not more than 7.5% of a fund's assets may be invested in a single enterprise, nor may a fund acquire more than 5% of the voting rights in any one concern.

Most Swiss investment trusts concentrate on specializing their investments. One may, for example, specialize in North American securities or another perhaps in European bonds. The real estate trust is somewhat of a Swiss specialty. Some 30% of the funds invested in investment trusts are invested in real estate trusts. The great majority of these real estate trusts invest right within Switzerland. In contrast the investment trusts that invest in securities do so mostly abroad. The size of the investment trusts as an institutional investor (their assets total 15 billion Swiss francs) makes them a force to be reckoned with on the international stock exchanges.

Giro System

There are essentially two giro or clearing systems in Switzerland. There are the giro accounts held by the major banks with the Swiss National Bank and there is the giro system of the Post Office, which serves the function of a check clearing institute.

The giro balances at the National Bank can be held by business firms, banks, individuals and governmental bodies. The National Bank reserves the right to accept or reject any application. There is a certain minimum balance that an account hold must maintain and the National Bank offers no interest on these accounts. As of the end of 1979 there were 16.6 billion Swiss francs in giro accounts held at the National Bank.*

Most of the major banks in Switzerland use the giro system of the National Bank to clear their interbank payments. The vast majority of giro payments are transfers from one giro account to another. All correspondents, agencies and branches of the National Bank accept and make payments for the accounts of giro customers free of charge. Banks making use of this system have no need to keep accounts with each other; transfers between banks can be made simply through the giro acounts. The banks which take advantage of their giro accounts in this way have formed a clearing group to supervise and insure their clearing transactions.

The giro system of the Post Office has evolved into a highly efficient means of making payments within Switzerland. The giro accounts at the Post Office have taken the place of what in the United States would be checking accounts. The payment of a bill for merchandise, travel expenses or hotel accommodations is almost never made by a bank check and seldom by credit card but rather through giro transfers in the Post Office. In nearly all cases when a bill is sent it is accompanied with a post office slip which can be used either as a giro transfer form or as a simple money order. If one uses the slip to make a giro transfer the Post Office will

*For comparison: Money supply M_1 = 22.6 billion SF (cash) + 45.8 billion SF (Sight deposits, inclusive of Giro accounts).

automatically debit the payee's account and transfer the funds to his creditor. If one of the parties involved in a business transaction does not have a giro account then he may simply send a postal money order.

The Post Office giro system also supplies the means by which Swiss can make deposits in their bank. The Post Office giro system and the giro system of the National Bank work in conjunction with each other to make transfer free of charge for customers of one system to customers of the other. It is therefore possible for businesses and individuals to make payments to any post office and then have it credited to their bank account.

A sculptured console on the Minister Cathedral in Berne.

CHAPTER 9

Banking Secrecy

Banking secrecy has become an issue of far reaching economic and political significance for the Swiss. As long as Swiss banks have administered secret accounts foreign governments have sought to pierce the veil of banking secrecy, and this trend will no doubt continue. On the one hand banking secrecy has done much to foster business for the Swiss banking industry, while on the other hand the concept of banking secrecy has made Switzerland the object of much political resentment. It cannot be denied that Swiss banks are an international haven for "laundering" funds. The number of cases in which this is true is certainly small; yet, though small in number, they give credence to the conceptualization of banking secrecy as a corrupting force. Swiss bankers have been forced into the position of having to develop a defensive attitude about their banking practices.

Such a defensive stand by the Swiss in regards to banking secrecy is by no means new. Banking secrecy has been for several centuries a cornerstone of Swiss banking practice; a tradition forged out of necessity and tested in time. The right to maintain a bank account secretly was seen as a personal right to privacy. Furthermore, as Switzerland had pledged itself to political neutrality the foreign holders of Swiss bank accounts were, it was felt, additionally entitled to expect from the Swiss an asylum for their property as well as their person.

During the 1930's foreign governments, and the National Socialist party in Germany in particular, had begun intensive campaigns of espionage to get at bank accounts held in Switzerland. Many methods were used and spies were event sent to work in Swiss banks in the hope of getting at certain account holders. For a time the invaders were quite successful. In Germany, for example, a number of Jews who had transferred their assets to Switzerland were forced to close out their accounts and repatriate their holdings. In light of these actions the Swiss government began to crack down on foreign agents and passed laws to discourage further espionage and protect foreigners who had accounts in Switzerland. Article 47 of the Swiss Federal Banking Law (1934, revised 1971) made it a criminal offense to break Swiss banking secrecy:

"1. Whoever divulges a secret entrusted to him in his capacity as officer, employee, authorized agent, liquidator or commissioner of a bank, as a representative of the Banking commission, officer or employee of a recognized auditing company, or whoever has become aware of such a secret in this capacity and whoever tries to induce others to violate professional secrecy, shall be punished by a prison term not to exceed six months or by a fine not exceeding SF 50,000.

"2. If the act has been committed by negligence, the penalty shall be a fine not exceeding SF 30,000.

"3. The violation of professional secrecy remains punishable even after termination of the official or employment relationship or the exercise of the profession.

"4. Federal and cantonal regulations concerning the obligation to testify and to furnish information to government authorities shall remain reserved."

Banks went even further in some cases to prevent the possibility of indiscretion for their clients by designating accounts only by numbers. The numbered account has no special legal status. They are covered by the same laws of banking secrecy that covers all accounts. The major difference is that the number of employees who know the identity of the account holder is limited to only the bank manager and two or three of his officers.

With the enactment of Article 47 (above) and Article 273 of the Swiss Criminal Code the criminal aspect of divulging banking secrecy was determined. The principles and limitations of banking secrecy, however, remain undefined. Typical of the Swiss mentality the confines of banking secrecy were left purposefully vague. After all, they would argue, if it is at all feasible to reach an understanding without writing it into law let us do so.

Domestically what is written into the federal fiscal law stipulates that bankers are obligated to testify in cases involving bankruptcy and criminal proceedings. It is further stipulated that under certain circumstances the bank may also have to furnish information in actions involving debt collection and inheritance. The obligation to furnish information in civil proceedings is dependent upon which canton has jurisdiction in the case.

Internationally the legal situation governing banking secrecy has evolved in a very different context. The limitations of banking secrecy are quite hazy and dependent on a number of political and economic factors. Abrogation of Swiss banking secrecy in its international context is achieved through mutual understanding of the courts, the government and the banks as to what constitutes a justifiable infringement on the rights of an account holder.

Switzerland is party to a host of multilateral treaties for legal assistance with other countries. Under these treaties the Swiss authorities promise to aid foreign governments in prosecuting a wide range of criminal cases. Such aid however, is forthcoming only if the crime the foreign government is prosecuting is also a crime under Swiss law. This fact has often led to misunderstandings and charges that the Swiss government is covering for its bankers; particularly in regard to tax matters. For example, in 1959 Switzerland was signatory to a treaty among members of the Council of Europe providing for reciprocal legal aid in criminal cases. However, Switzerland made it clear that violations of foreign exchange regulations or foreign tax laws (unless there was fraud) and offences against foreign military laws were not to be included, as those are not considered crimes in Switzerland.

In Switzerland tax evasion—that is the failure to declare or pay taxes, is not considered a crime. In the United States where the legal system is based on English common law, tax evasion is a crime. Swiss tax law sees it as a responsibility of the taxpayer to file a proper return. The constitutional concept of a relationship between the state and the Swiss citizen prohibits the government from demanding information from banks for finding undeclared assets.

Under Swiss law, then, tax evasion is not a criminal offense and is only punishable by a penal tax. Tax fraud, however, is considered a criminal offense and so in those cases where a foreign government can prove tax fraud the Swiss authorities are obligated to provide information on the accused's bank account. The line between tax evasion and tax fraud has to be determined in a court of law. According to the authorities in Bern the border-line is drawn as follows:

> "Tax fraud encompasses the use of false, forged or intrin-sically untrue information, such as falsified books of account, balance sheets, profit and loss statements or payroll records, and other data provided by third parties, with the intent to mislead the tax authorities."

In the absence of international treaties the Swiss have taken the position that no information or assistance is to be granted for matters involving the collection of foreign taxes. The Swiss con-sider it the responsibility of foreign governments to find internal means to get their taxes paid.

Where international tax treaties exist, (for example, the Swiss-American treaty governing mutual assistance in the prosecution of criminals) Switzerland has agreed to the exchange of informa-tion for tax purposes. This treaty in particular was aimed at undermining internationally organized crime. Swiss practice in meeting the demands of such treaties has been somewhat inconsistent. The treaties themselves are quite unpopular among the Swiss as it is felt to infringe on an age-old tradition of personal liberty and banking tradition. Additionally one must realize the importance of the banking industry in Switzerland and the large amount of foreign capital that it attracts. Swiss banking secrecy and, in particular, the unique provisions of Swiss tax law are very good for business. A large segment of the Swiss economy has been built upon the favorable tax climate and liberal free market policies.

In the latest Swiss American Treaty named above, the Swiss government has in effect, through careful wording of the document, reserved the final right as to whether or not they will disclose information. In the case of X vs. Eidgenossische Steuerver-waltung, the Swiss Federal Court determined that the Swiss bank involved was obligated to provide as much information to American authorities as the bank would have to provide local cantonal authorities if they were prosecuting the case.[1] However, in fact, the information that the Swiss are willing to provide is probably substantially less than the American expectations of what they will get. Swiss bankers are hesitant to provide unilateral assistance to the United States as other governments would undoubtedly want the same. Again in the case of X vs. Eidgenossische Steurverwaltung the decision by the Federal court determined that the professional secrets of doctors, lawyers and priests remain protected in any case. In a domestic case in Zürich it was decided that lawyers, acting as trustees for their clients, could not be compelled to reveal information about such acts. It would be quite an extraordinary ruling that would demand Swiss disclosures in a tax case where an American used a lawyer as his go-between with a Swiss bank.[2]

Most recently, in the wake of the Chiasso Affair, Swiss banks once again made efforts to clean up their image. The Swiss Bankers Association in conjunction with the National Bank drew up a gentlemen's agreement to further "demystify" banking secrecy. No longer (as of June 1977), are banks to be accepting accounts from anonymous customers hiding behind the faces of their lawyers. In this new agreement banks specify that they will only accept accounts if they can identify the legitimacy of the actual holder. Section IV of this agreement further states that:

Article 8   "A bank will not actively aid capital transfers from foreign countries in violation of those countries' laws . . ."

Article 9   "A bank will not issue incomplete and misleading documents that support customers' attempts to violate the laws of their own countries, in particular the tax laws."

In effect this agreement does not really say anything new. Swiss banks were never anxious to become involved in any type of criminal case. Certainly the identification of new customers had always been standard banking practice. In the future, as it has been in the past, Swiss banking secrecy will remain an institution of considerable worth. As an ideological issue banking secrecy will continue to be underplayed in favor of its more pragmatic aspects. The majority of Swiss people stand behind the concept of banking secrecy; they realize the important role banking secrecy has played in attracting foreign capital and making Switzerland into the international financial center that it is. Politically, too, banking secrecy is intrinsically caught up in Switzerland's position of neutrality. In the Swiss vision of neutrality Switzerland is seen as an absolute asylum against unjust foreign laws which infringe on the rights of the individual. As one Swiss professor put it, "The individual has a right to discretion—

ultimately also in his financial afffairs—and when this right is violated, something is lost that in essence belongs to the freedom of the individual." [3] When the public interest is judged by the Swiss to be clearly greater than the rights of the individual banking secrecy will be lifted by the authorities. But in all other cases it is doubtful that the Swiss will ever compromise banking secrecy, whether or not a treaty exists.

To better understand the distinction between the public interest and the rights of the individual let us consider two recent cases.

The Shah of Iran

The case of the Shah has focused much attention on the accommodation of Swiss Banking law. After the Shah fled Iran the new Islamic government sent a representative to Bern to ask Swiss authorities to freeze the assets of the Shah in Switzerland. They argued that the Shah was a criminal and that the funds he and his family had in Switzerland should be returned to the Iranian people. The Swiss authorities agreed to consider the matter.

Several weeks later they issued results of a study undertaken to determine what amount of funds that left Iran had eventually reached Switzerland. Comparing the holdings of Iran residents, corporate bodies, and the central bank the Swiss found the following:

TABLE 3
Iranian Assets

As of (1978)	January	December
	(in millions of Sfr.)	
Iranian assets held by banks	927	1038
Iranian funds held in fiduciary accounts	855	926

Clearly not much had reached the Swiss since the revolution according to these figures. Iranian officials viewed the results skeptically as they estimated the Shah alone had transferred some 15 billion US dollars in his last months in power. They again pressed the Swiss authorities for action.

Under Swiss banking secrecy law, however, the only conditions under which the Swiss authorities could consider repatriating the funds brought out by the Shah would be if the Shah could be proven guilty of conduct that was considered criminal both under Swiss as well as Iranian law. The burden of proving this guilt would be up to the Iranian authorities. Political crises in Iran are not a criminal offense as seen by Swiss law.

To date the Iranian officials have yet to find out from the Swiss if the Shah even has an account in Switzerland. Iranian officials still have not been able to produce evidence sufficient to satisfy the Swiss legal authorities that the Shah is a criminal. In fact it now appears that the Iranian government has just about given up hope for seizing these assets in Switzerland. The Iranian ambassador in Switzerland recently commented that even if the Shah had assets in Switzerland most of them would probably be moved out before the Iranians could act.

Swiss banking secrecy has, we can assume, been very effective for the Shah. Banking secrecy in this case was clearly called into use under the guidelines set out by the law. In our next case the protection of Swiss banking secrecy was not so clear cut.

US Securities and Exchange Commission versus The Progress Group

This case is well known among bankers in Switzerland as it caused the Swiss banking industry considerable embarrassment. The embarrassment stems not so much from the way the Swiss banking commission handled the case but rather from the fact that the case received considerable negative publicity. At issue is whether or not Swiss banking secrecy was compromised. The bankers in Switzerland will adamantly deny that banking secrecy was weakened by SEC pressure while Col. Harwood and the Progress Group are quite determined that a Swiss Bank actually violated banking secrecy by giving out the names of its account holders to the SEC. The truth probably lies somewhere between these two extremes. Certainly the manner in which the Swiss bank involved handled the case was somewhat irregular and indicates that they were under considerable stress from U.S. pressure.

The Progress Group was made up of U.S. investors who, through entities like Mondial Commercial Ltd. in Lugano, invested in gold coins and later gold bullion and South African gold shares through Credit Swiss in Zürich. Col. E.C. Harwood of the American Institute for Economic Research acted as their adviser in these investments. The accounts totalling nearly $100 million U.S. were kept in what could best be described as a pooled account of Credit Swiss. Although the accounts were under the name of the Progress Group and related firms Col. Harwood has evidence that several officers at Credit Swiss undoubtedly also knew the identity of some if not all of the ultimate account holders.

The SEC stepped into the picture when it feared that US investors were not being adequately protected. The administration of the accounts by the Progress Group was not in order according to the SEC. Furthermore, they felt that Col. Harwood was acting improperly by advising the purchase of South African gold mining shares. Col. Harwood was not registered with the NASD or SEC.

The SEC approached the Swiss banking commission and Credit Swiss asking for more information in regard to the status of the account holders. At this point interest groups began to play a larger role and motivations for preservation led the Swiss banks into a compromising position.

The legal history of the case is long and complicated. In very much simplified form the following occurred:

1. The SEC demanded information from Credit Swiss; no doubt reminding the management of Credit Swiss in the process that in the interest of the bank's extensive business assets in the US they should respond promptly.

2. Credit Swiss either in panic or as a result of poor legal advice agreed to extend a $120 million letter of credit to the banking authorities in New York. This was to assure the banking authorities that the assets of the Progress Group were safely being held by the bank. This action also admitted to U.S. jurisdiction in a matter of Swiss banking secrecy.

3. After a prolonged court battle the Swiss banking commission, the SEC, and the Progress Group agreed that names of the account holders would be given out by Credit Swiss under the following conditions (from the Banking Commission Decree 1976):

If   a) Fraud or misrepresentation has occurred in connection with the specific investments with which the investors were involved.

        b) The investor gives written consent to have his name divulged.

        c) Information will be provided on investors whose identities are already in the possession of the SEC.

4. The SEC obtained a list of account holders. Two sources are possible: The SEC obtained the names in files they seized from the Progress Group in the U.S.; the names were given to the SEC by Credit Swiss.

    In either case the SEC ultimately took no action against account holders and neither did the IRS as far as we know.

5. The SEC suit with Col. Harwood was settled. Col. Harwood agreed to abstain from any further participation in the purchase or sale of securities and agreed not to act as a broker or dealer in securities. The customers of the Progress Group were given the option of keeping their assets with Credit Swiss or transferring them elsewhere.

As the case progressed it was clear that the SEC did not have a very strong case against Col. Harwood although the Progress Group certainly was on the threshold as to whether or not they complied with SEC regulations.

What interests us are points 1, 2, and 4 above. The secrecy of the Progress Group customers certainly was imperilled, but was Swiss banking secrecy violated? Only in the event of criminal conduct, such as fraud, should any information have been released or an account relationship admitted. This was clearly not the case here.

Credit Swiss was ill-advised to put up a letter of credit with the banking authorities in New York. The United States had no clear-cut jurisdiction in this case up to that point. Under normal circumstances the Swiss bank would have refused any involvement until U.S. authorities could have produced sufficient evidence to begin legal proceedings. The conditions here, however, were anything but normal. The account at Credit Swiss was in the name of the Progress Group, not in the name of the individual clients. Credit Swiss interest in maintaining good relations with U.S. authorities put them under a strain to cooperate where possible, and Credit Swiss officials were uncertain of their own relation with the Progress Group and the SEC.

Bank officials at Credit Swiss say they did all they could to protect the Progress Group until the Swiss banking commission moved in to clear up the situation. Reading the decree of the banking commission however, it is quite obvious that they were acting on behalf of the SEC. In such matters of international law in which there was no clear-cut course to take the Swiss could easily have opted to take no action as, for example, we saw was the case with the Shah of Iran. In the Progress Group case officials of the banking commission say that the accounts were in such disorder that they had to do something. That may well be but you can be assured that if the SEC had not been involved and if the Swiss banks were not so worried about their image vis-à-vis the U.S. authorities this whole affair would have been solved through internal means.

In the aftermath of this affair Credit Swiss has signed a secret agreement with the SEC regarding their business relationship with U.S. clients and this, too, is indicative of the anxiety they felt.

However, as far as Credit Swiss actually divulging the name of the account holders in the Progress Group, lawyers on both sides deny this has ever occurred. More likely the SEC was able to reconstruct the names of the account holders out of files seized from the American Institute Counselors Inc. in the U.S. and then present them to Credit Swiss for verification as stipulated in the Swiss banking commission decree.

In retrospect we can say that banking secrecy was compromised in so far as a U.S. governmental authority was recognized by a Swiss bank in a case in which they should have had no jurisdiction. The lesson to be learned is not that Swiss banking agency has been broken, but rather that the Swiss banks, too, are influenced by economic and political pressures. For those very concerned about banking secrecy this is not very reassuring, but it is doubtful a Swiss bank would under similar circumstances act imprudently again. For the future both Swiss banks and foreign account holders should be more wary of the influence of foreign authorities and business interests.

CHAPTER 10

The Swiss National Bank

Structure and Administration

The establishment of a National Bank in Switzerland was founded upon the Federal Law of October 6, 1905. Before the National Bank began its activities on June 20, 1907, there were some thirty-six private and cantonal institutions which up to that time had been controlling the supply of bank notes.

The Swiss National Bank has two headquarters, one in Bern, the other in Zürich. While the National Bank's offices in Bern function to serve the legal and administrative needs of the Bank, the other offices in Zürich house the Bank's directorate. The National Bank also has branch offices in eight other towns (Aarau, Basle, St. Gallen, Geneva, Lausanne, Luzern, Lugano, and Neuchâtel) to conduct the National Bank's business in these areas.

The basic provisions of law which support and control the National Bank in its role as a central administrator and note issuer are contained in Article 39 of the Federal Constitution (amended 1951), and in the National Bank Law of December 23, 1953.

In essence the Swiss National Bank is organized as a corporation: Swiss citizens, Swiss companies incorporated under public law, and corporate bodies who have their head offices in Switzerland may register as stockholders of the National Bank. The Federal government does not own any part of the Bank's capital, although it does have the statutory power to exert decisive influence on the composition of the Bank authorities and the Bank's management. Of the 25 million Swiss frances of paid-in capital (1/3 of the total share capital allotted) over half is held by cantons and cantonal banks. Apart from the cantons and other public bodies there are also over 5,000 private shareholders.

All shareholders are entitled to take part in the General Meeting of shareholders which takes place yearly in Bern. Every share entitles the holder to one vote. A private shareholder may not, however, cast more than one hundred votes on behalf of his own shares or those he represents. Although the shareholders in their General Meeting along with the Bank authorities and Bank management are the National Bank's controlling authorities, the powers of the shareholders are quite limited, owing to the special public nature of the bank. During a typical meeting, the shareholders will receive the annual report and the year's accounts (after they have been approved by the Federal Government). They will elect the Committee of Auditors and, when necessary, the shareholders have the responsibility of designating fifteen of the members on the Bank Council. If at a General Meeting any proposals for changes in the National Bank are made, they must be submitted to the Federal Government and the Federal Parliament for approval. Also at the General Meetings the net profit of the National Bank is allocated according to the formula prescribed by law.

The Bank Council

Another controlling authority of the National Bank, as previously mentioned, is the Bank Council. The Council is composed of 40 members, twenty five are appointed by the Federal government and the remaining fifteen by the shareholders. The election requirements for this Council have been written in such a way as to safeguard the bank from political and geographical influences. Members must represent various sectors of the economy and diverse parts of the country. The Bank Council is generally responsible for supervising the conduct of the Bank's business. The Bank Council chooses new members of the Bank Executive Committee, appoints the Local Committees, and proposes new members to the Directorate. The Bank Council is also responsible for presenting the National Bank's financial statements in their final form, for fixing the denomination of notes to be issued, for withdrawing notes from circulation and for deciding upon the establishment of branches.

The Bank Executive Committee

The Bank Executive Committee, which is made up of ten members of the Bank Council (including the Chairman and Vice Chairman), is responsible for a more detailed supervision of the Bank. This Committee must meet at least once a month and has the duty to discuss all matters that the Bank Council must handle. The Bank Executive Committee also advises on fixing the official discount rate. The Bank Executive Committee is in close touch with the Bank's Directorate and acts as a liaison between the Bank Council and the Board of Directors.

Other controlling committees include the Committee of Auditors and the Local Committees. The Committee of Auditors is the chief auditing agency of the shareholders. They submit a written report to the General Meeting of the shareholders in which they discuss their audit of the annual accounts and the balance sheet. The Committee of Auditors is free to examine any aspect of the National Bank's business and is also responsible for keeping the Federal Government apprised of the National Bank's business activities.

The Local Committees are made up of representatives of the business community in the individual banking districts. They serve as an advisory board to express opinions to the National Bank's Board of Directors. Additionally the local committees may recommend managers for National Bank branches and can supervise the loan policies of their individual bank offices.

Management

The Board of Directors (Direktorium) is the supreme managing and executive body in the National Bank. The Board is made up of three members each of whom is chosen by the Federal Government. This Board of Directors, along with their deputies, is directly responsible for overseeing and determining the policy of the National Bank.

The Board of Directors has it as their specific duty to fix the official discount rate and the interest rate on loans. They also are responsible for organizing, under the direction of the Bank Council and the Bank Committee, the credit and monetary policy. They carefully monitor, like the Board of Governors of the Federal Reserve in the U.S., the condition of the money and capital markets in order to determine the state of the economy. The Board of Directors is also responsible for representing the National Bank to outside parties. The President of the Board, in particular, represents the National Bank to all outsiders unless some other member is commissioned to do so. Finally the Board of Directors is responsible for selection of many of the officers and employees of the National Bank's head offices.

Each of the three members of the Board of Directors is the head of a Department in the National Bank. The President of the Board is in charge of Department One, which determines overall policy of the National Bank. Department Two, which has its headquarters in Bern, is responsible for administrative dealings, the management of gold reserves and the issuance of bank notes. Department Three, again in Zürich, regulates foreign exchange and international payment transactions.

Each branch office of the National Bank is headed by a local director, or branch manager, who is elected by the Federal Government on the recommendation of the Bank Council for a period of six years. This manager must follow the policies set forth by the National Bank's Board of Directors and for activities beyond the normal course of operations, the branch manager must go to the Board of Directors for approval.

Duties and Activities of the Swiss National Bank

Under the Swiss Constitution, the exclusive right to issue bank notes belongs to the National Bank. The Bank may only issue bank notes against holdings of gold and gold convertible currencies or against certain types of short term assets. The National Bank is required to have gold backing for at least 40% of the notes in circulation.

At present, the Swiss National Bank holds gold valued at about ll.9 billion Swiss francs,* and the amount of Swiss francs circulating is 21.3 billion, so the National Bank is well within its legal limits.° If one were to include its foreign currency holdings then Switzerland has well over 100% backing for its franc.

In April of 1978 the Federal Government began consideration of a bill which would do away with the National Bank's obligation to maintain a 40% gold backing for the Swiss franc. Many government officials feel that the 40% law is "archaic." They say they do not see a need for the National Bank to purchase gold whenever the money supply is increased, especially as gold prices may be temporarily inflated at that time. Despite the opinion of government legislators, however, such a bill would require a national referendum and the traditional Swiss would probably be quite hesitant to endorse such a bill. Three years ago, over a similar issue, the Swiss rejected a government proposal to revise the Swiss National Bank's regulations.

Since September 1936 when the Swiss franc was last devalued, the National Bank has no longer had an obligation to redeem its notes in gold. However, the National Bank is still responsible for ensuring that the Swiss franc exchange rate stays within a band of fluctuation of the gold parity as determined by the Federal Council. As of January 1973, the official link between the U.S. dollar and the Swiss franc was abrogated in order to give the National Bank a greater hold on the domestic money supply. Later in that year all the major European currencies were "floating". In a relatively short time the exchange rate of currencies, like the U.S. dollar, fell far below their theoretical parities. The rates on the Swiss foreign exchange markets were allowed to freely follow the forces of supply and demand. Through all this, however, the legal gold parity of the Swiss franc has been maintained by the National Bank (.21759 m.g. gold/ Swiss franc + or -2.5%).

In order to be able to act determinately, and with flexibility, the National Bank has found it necessary to limit the scope of its operations to the short term. The specific operations which the National Bank is allowed to engage in are specified in the National Bank Law. Following is a list of the principal operational duties of the Swiss National Bank:

°valued at rate of approximately $97 U.S./ounce.

l. *Issuance of Notes:*

As already mentioned the National Bank has the exclusive right to issue notes. The Bank's main responsibility is to supervise the money circulation and to promulgate an economic policy that will be to the benefit of the country. The National Bank can withdraw notes from circulation only with the consent of the Federal Government.

2. *Acceptance of Money Deposits:*

The National Bank accepts deposits from banks, private firms and even individuals, although they are not allowed to pay any interest on these accounts. There is an exception to this: balances of the Cantons and Federal Government do receive interest payments from their accounts with the National Bank.

3. *Discounting:*

The National Bank will re-discount bills and cheques that have a maturity date not exceeding three months. Most frequently bills drawn in connection with commercial transactions are used for this type of discount.

4. *Foreign Transactions:*

The National Bank is authorized to buy and sell foreign bills and checks as long as their maturity is under three months. Most of the National Bank's investments abroad are either Treasury bills, bank acceptances or sight deposits with foreign central banks.

5. *Securities Dealings:*

The Bank is authorized to deal in the longer term bills and bonds of the Federal government and the cantons. The National Bank can also handle the sales and purchases of securities for the account of others. (Understandably for their own account, they are actively engaged in the purchase and sale of gold). They also may grant current account advances against bonds, Federal Debt Register claims, discountable bills and gold as collateral.

6. Giro and Clearing:

One of the most important duties of the Swiss National Bank is to insure the smooth functioning of the country's collection systems. We have in a previous section already discussed the giro system in which the National Bank acts as a clearing house for money and audit transfers. Settlement can take place quite efficiently through the system particularly when it is used in conjunction with the giro system of the Post Office. The National Bank also directs and participates in the security clearing done by the banks. Cash settlements for securities sold on the stock exchanges are made through clearing offices which credit or debit the necessary giro accounts at the National Bank.

The National Bank is also responsible for collection activities. In most cases members of clearing offices will present the bank with checks and matured bills that have been drawn on other clearing firms.

7. Control over Security Issues:

Although domestic bond and share issues are not subject to authorization in Switzerland, the National Bank must be informed of all foreign issues. Thanks to the stability of the Swiss government, the strength of the Swiss franc and the capital inflows which give Switzerland so much liquidity, foreign governments and corporations are quite eager to borrow money on the Swiss market. The National Bank, however, must carefully judge the effect of floating a bond issue on the Swiss economy as a whole. Since the economy is rather small, the National Bank must weigh the consequences of every bond issue. After examining the money and capital market conditions, the Bank may decide that a foreign bond issue may have an adverse effect on the money supply or the interest rate and veto the issue.

8. Extraordinary powers

From time to time the Federal Government empowers the National Bank through an executive decree to assume more power than it would normally have. The decrees give the Bank temporary power to deal with unusual or crisis situations. We shall discuss the scope and contents of such decrees in our examination of the National Bank's instruments of control.

Relations of the National Bank with Other Banks

The relation of the Swiss National Bank with the banks in Switzerland is really quite unique. Communication between most banks and the National Bank is very good; yet, the banks of Switzerland enjoy considerable freedom of 'both control and supervision from their central bank. Unlike most other central banks the Swiss National Bank has no legal right to direct or supervise the banks' activities. Thus, for the majority of Swiss bankers, the National Bank is seen more as an adviser than as a leader. Cooperation is the key word to describe the relation between the National Bank and the commercial banks. Major decisions made by the National Bank's Directorate are made with the advice and consent of the leading Swiss bankers. As we have already seen, the Swiss are historically adverse to writing anything into law that can be accomplished through mutual understanding and compromise. The National Bank is able to effectively influence banks' business operations by obtaining their voluntary cooperation through gentlemen's agreements. We will examine these gentlemen's agreements in their role as an instrument of control in the next section.

In its international dealings with other central banks the Swiss National Bank is probably best known for the role it plays with the Bank for International Settlements (B.I.S). The B.I.S. was founded in 1930 to further cooperation between the various central banks and to supply additional facilities for international financial operations. The headquarters of the B.I.S. are in Basle. The Swiss National Bank, as it does not participate in the International Monetary Fund, uses the B.I.S. as a springboard for many of its international exchange transactions. Switzerland, for example, arranges its swap agreements with the United States through the B.I.S.

Balance Sheet of the Swiss National Bank
January 5, 1979

Assets

	(in millions of francs)
Gold Holdings	11,903.9
Foreign Currency	32,047.2
Foreign Bonds in Swiss francs	1,981.0
Domestic Portfolio	
Bills	235.8
Government Bonds	—
Lombard advances (against collateral)	10.4
Open-Market Paper	348.0
Domestic Correspondents (Banks with which the Swiss National does business)	70.5
Other Assets	74.1
Total	46,670.9

Liabilities

Own funds (share capital and legal reserves)	70.0
Notes in circulation	21,619.4
Liabilities due at sight	
Giro accounts	16,331.3
Other	4,444.3
Term liabilities:	
sterilization rescriptions	3,403.7
Other Liabilities	1,802.2
Total	46,670.9

St. Germain's fountain, Geneva, Switzerland

CHAPTER 11

Swiss National Bank Capital Controls

Within the last few years there has been much discussion of a revision in the National Bank law to give the Swiss National Bank a more sophisticated and diversified control of the monetary and fiscal policy in Switzerland. The instruments of control now available to the National Bank are, for the most part, based on emerging legislation. Economic conditions in Switzerland have been strongly influenced by changing international influences and the Swiss National Bank, to be effective, has had to make use of control instruments as variable as the external factors which have been effecting the economy. The National Bank Act of 1953 which empowered the National Bank under ordinary law to discount bills, make lombard advances (loans granted on collateral securities) and to engage in open market operations, is, by itself, not equal to providing the National Bank with sufficient control over the country's monetary policy.

In recent years, for example, Switzerland has been experiencing large scale capital in-flows and substantial balance of payments surplus on current account. These surpluses have a tendency to bring about excessive increases in the supply of money and credit throughout the economy. The National Bank, to combat this tendency, has followed a course of monetary policy that 1) is aimed at reducing the inflow of undesirable foreign funds, 2) encourages reinvestment abroad of foreign funds, 3) tries to sterilize the inflows where possible and, 4) puts direct restrictions on domestic credit expansion. In order to do this the National Bank has had to rely on government cooperation and the support of the banks, as discount rate policy and open market operations are not effective enough instruments, in Switzerland, to give the needed control. Hence, we see the National Bank being granted a number of extraordinary powers by emergency legislation and gentlemen's agreements with the banks.

The fact that the Swiss have been so successful in controlling inflation (2.1%) and unemployment (.5%) illustrates,[*] in part, the effectiveness of the National Bank in achieving a slow but steady growth in the money supply along with their ability to maintain a conservative credit policy. In this chapter we will consider the instruments of control which make the Swiss National Bank a successful central bank, but it is important to keep in mind the unique character of the Swiss mentality and economic structure which helps to make monetary policy as effective as it is.

Gentlemen's Agreements

Gentlemen's Agreements fundamentally are institutionalized control through compromise and cooperation. They represent Swiss banks' willingness to voluntarily agree to giving the National Bank additional means of control on a temporary basis in order to help it perform its economic functions.

The first Gentlemen's Agreement was concluded in 1927 when banks agreed to notify the central bank when they proposed to issue a foreign loan. Since then there have been a large number of gentlemen's agreements circulated, most directed at controlling the credit conditions in Switzerland. In recent years these agreements have empowered the National Bank to call in minimum reserves on increases in deposits, to impose quantitative restrictions on lending to domestic borrowers (suspended in Spring 1975), and to impose an interest ban (and commission levy) on foreign Swiss franc deposits.

The success of the gentlemen's agreements lies in the voluntary nature of their enactment. Once a problem in a particular area has been recognized, the National Bank will get together with leaders in the banking community to discuss how the situation can best be resolved. When an agreement is reached, it is put in the form of a letter and sent out to the other banks in Switzerland. They sign the agreement and pledge to voluntarily abide by the rules set out in the agreement.

The National Bank cannot openly take punitive actions against

[*]1978 figures.

any bank that would renege on such an agreement, but there are subtle pressures within the banking system that make such an event unlikely. Remember, it is the major banks along with the National Bank that have formulated the agreements. Enforcement of the agreements, if not possible through the political pressure of the National Bank, is often insured by the economic pressures of the big banks.

For example, towards the end of 1977 a gentlemen's agreement was signed by most all of the banks which stipulated that Swiss banks could no longer have their agents pick up foreign currencies in countries with capital export restrictions. From that point on if for example an Italian wanted to transfer his holdings to Switzerland, it would be his responsibility to arrange for the funds to arrive in Switzerland. To enforce such an agreement is obviously a very difficult affair, especially since the Swiss banks have been doing quite well in this business for a long time. Certainly in many cases the Swiss banks still make these pick-ups but on the whole they have made an effort to cut down on such transactions. In a case where a signator to such an agreement openly violated the spirit of the understanding, officials at the larger banks and the National Bank could sanction them by subtle business (poor exchange rate quotations) or political pressures (have them called to the National Bank for a talk); if there is widespread dissension on an agreement it obviously will fail.

Swiss banks are willing to voluntarily concede power to the National Bank because they realize that their long—term interests are served best by the National Bank's efforts to keep the economy sound and the currency stable. The teamwork system that has developed between the commercial banks and the National Banks enables the authorities to intervene efficiently, even during changing situations. Such a system may only be possible in Switzerland where the country is so small that agreement can quickly be reached through compromise.

The widespread use of the gentlemen's agreements in Switzerland gives the National Bank an added measure of flexibility in its means of economic control. Apart from such gentlemen's agreements and the National Bank Law of 1953, the Swiss National Bank also is given special powers by Federal decrees. These Federal decrees give legal backing on a temporary basis, to central bank instruments that had often previously been made functional by voluntary agreements. Until a new National Bank law is passed these Federal decrees will have to provide the National Bank with the chief means by which they can pursue their monetary policy.

While the Parliament and National Bank representatives are still working on a new all-encompassing National Bank Law, the National Bank is successfully pursuing its monetary policy with the help of this stop gap legislation. By manipulating the monetary base through their temporary instruments of control the National Bank has managed to maintain relative control of the money supply despite inflows of foreign capital and fluctuations in the exchange rate. Following is a list of the instruments of monetary policy used by the National Bank and a summary of how they influence the monetary base. In subsequent pages we consider how these instruments interact to produce the monetary policy sought by the National Bank.

TABLE 4. Instruments of the Swiss National Bank*

Instrument	Component of the Monetary Base influenced:
Purchase and Sale of foreign currencies Conversion Requirement for Capital Export Settlement of long term $/SF Swaps Settlement of SF Swaps	Variation in Foreign Currency reserves (CR)
Purchase and Sale of Securities	Variations in Open market portfolio (OM)

Minimum reserve requirements for
  Domestic and Foreign Accounts
Limit on Credit Expansion
Sterilization of Money on the State's
  account at the National Bank
Issuance of short term (6-12 month)
  Sterilization rescriptions
	Variation in the Reserve component (RC)

Discount credit policy
Lombard credit policy
Settlement of short term $/SF Swaps
Discounting and retirement of Sterilization
  rescriptions
Stand-by credit of the State for commercial
  banks
	Variation in the Volume of Refinancing (RF)

*Adapted from a report to the Direktorium of the National Bank, October 1977.

Of the above components that influence the monetary base, the National Bank has a direct means of control over all but the volume of refinancing. Seen in equation form the monetary base is influenced by the National Bank through the sum of its components. Monetary Base $(B) = (CR + OM + RC + RF)$. It is the goal of the National Bank to control the monetary base, and therefore the money supply, as closely as possible.

Growth in M_1 and Monetary Base 1976-1979

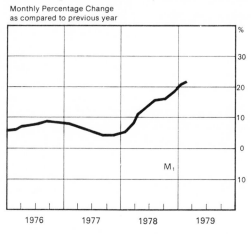

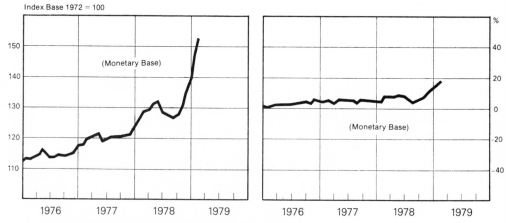

The chief reason for controlling the monetary base is to keep the price level fairly constant through the maintenance of a slow but steady growth in the money supply. At present the National Bank estimates that an increase of about 5% per annum in the monetary base would be an ideal growth rate. Although the Swiss National Bank is no more capable of maintaining this rate than other central banks they have had more success in meeting these goals because of a number of external circumstances which have been working in their favor. The days of fine tuning the monetary base through careful manipulation of control instruments have not yet arrived. But Switzerland does show that sensible monetary policy coupled with widespread fiscal cooperation can keep the goals of economic policy in sight.

Percentage changes in Consumer and Wholesale Prices

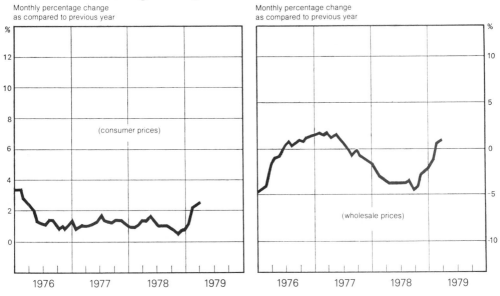

Monthly percentage change
as compared to previous year

(consumer prices)

Monthly percentage change
as compared to previous year

(wholesale prices)

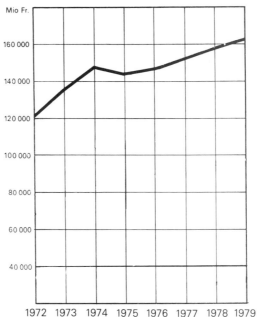

Development of GNP
in Millions of Swiss Francs

This, however, is only part of the picture. The monetary policy of the National Bank has many far-reaching effects on the banking system as a whole. Manipulation of the monetary base has a profound effect on the liquidity of the bank system. The short to medium term effect is on the money and capital markets. Over the longer term the exchange rate is also influenced. When considering Swiss economic policy such factors that would influence the exchange rates are of paramount important. The exchange rate is central to National Bank monetary policy as Switzerland's economic, political and geographical position puts her at the center of an interdependent world. Variations in the foreign exchange rate of the Swiss franc are key indicators of how National Bank policy is working. As we begin to examine in depth the components of the monetary base we will see that the most useful instruments of the central bank are those relating to the exchange rate.

1. Monetary Reserves

The monetary reserves of the National Bank are made up of the Bank's holdings of gold and foreign currencies minus the credit balance of foreign and central banks which hold their accounts at the National Bank. When speaking of monetary reserves one really only has to consider changes in the amount of foreign currency holdings, as the gold holdings of the National Bank have been quite constant in the last few years.

The easiest way for the National Bank to effect its holdings of foreign currencies is through direct intervention on the foreign exchange markets. In recent years the National Bank has found itself forced into this position periodically. People from abroad have been investing quite heavily in Switzerland and this along with several other factors has led to a substantial appreciation of the Swiss franc. So that their important export industries will not be priced out of the market the National Bank has found it necessary to intervene in an attempt to slow the appreciation of the franc. As the National Bank buys up foreign currencies the demand for these currencies rises so that their price will rise as their worth relative to the Swiss franc increases.

An additional effect of this purchase of foreign currencies is an increase in the supply of Swiss francs. The commercial banks holding the Swiss francs that were paid out by the National Bank now find themselves with excess francs. They respond by increasing their demand for Swiss franc investment opportunities (i.e. domestic). The effect of this is to lower domestic interest rates.

Remembering Switzerland's very close relationship with the international money markets we must extend this consideration of foreign currency purchases a bit farther. After the domestic interest rates begin to decrease it becomes more attractive for the commercial banks to look abroad for investment. Also as interest rates go down in Switzerland foreigners find it less attractive to invest in Switzerland. The level to which domestic interest rates will fall is dependent upon the portfolios that the commercial banks want to hold. If, for example, the Swiss are wary of investing abroad and so hold a larger share of their investments domestically, then, when the National Bank intervenes on the foreign exchange market, domestic interest rates would fall farther than if domestic and foreign investments were freely interchangeable. Note also that the lower Swiss interest rates go the less likely foreigners are to invest in Switzerland and hence the demand for Swiss francs decreases. The Swiss franc foreign exchange rate is a function of interest rates as well as a function of tthe demand for foreign currencies.

National Bank action when intervening on the foreign exchange markets is most often in opposition to their plans for monetary policy. With funds flowing into Switzerland, as has been happening in recent years, Swiss banks have been finding themselves with greater and greater liquidity. Looking at the big banks, for example, their liquid assets: cash on hand, credit balances on drawing accounts, and balances in postal check accounts, amounted to 4.8 billion or roughly 9% of total assets in 1968; in 1978 their liquid assets were 18.9 billion Swiss francs. As the larger capital inflows continue the National Bank must try to reduce the effects these excess reserves will have on the growth of money supply. In order to do this the National Bank makes use of a number of instruments including swaps, conversion requirements for capital export and sterilizing rescriptions.

One time arsenal, this 17th century building in the old town of Geneva now houses the Cantonal Archives.

In 1962 the Federal Reserve set up the first swap agreement with the Bank of France for 450 million. Since then the swap network has grown until today the credit lines for swaps total more than $30 billion. For the Swiss National Bank they have become an important instrument of control. The short term swaps which are a very effective means of controlling liquidity in the domestic economy will be discussed in a later section. Here, however, we want to consider the longer term and SF/$ swaps and their effects.

The long term swaps have a maturity of between one to three months. They are made to stabilize what central bank officials call "disorderly" foreign exchange markets. In a typical swap agreement the Federal Reserve agrees to buy dollars from a commercial bank (Chase, Citibank) with Swiss francs it will borrow from the Swiss National Bank. The Fed cables the Swiss National Bank and they in turn credit the Fed's account with Swiss francs. Following the Fed's instructions they pay the Swiss francs to a West German commercial bank that will, in turn, pay Citibank or Chase. In effect, the Federal Reserve borrows Swiss francs from the National Bank to create upward pressure on the dollar.

At the same time the Federal Reserve will credit the Swiss National Bank account with dollars for the Swiss francs it obtained. If the National Bank does not immediately need the dollars it can invest them in a nonmarketable security of the United States Treasury.

The Federal Reserve agrees to repay in three months the Swiss francs they have borrowed. The Fed can acquire the francs either in the market place or from a foreign central bank. If the currency markets have not stabilized by the time the three months are up, the Fed can simply renew the swap. The Swiss National Bank is protected from exchange rate fluctuations; it is the Fed that will make a profit or loss on the deal.

Through their long term swaps the Swiss National Bank temporarily affects the monetary base. Commercial banks in Switzerland which received Swiss francs from the Federal Reserve in exchange for their dollars can only take advantage of their Swiss franc liquidity as long as the swap is in effect. If the banks do not expect the swaps to be renewed they are unlikely to make any substantial changes in their investment portfolios. The long run effect on interest rates is slight if it exists at all. It is interesting to speculate whether these long term swaps can have any appreciable effect on the exchange rates at all. After all, if there are no interest rate adjustments in response to the swap agreements, then we must doubt if exchange rates will ever respond to swaps.

We also want to consider here the SF/$ swap as an instrument. In this type of swap the Swiss National Bank can intervene on behalf of the Swiss franc exchange rate and cut back simultaneously its currency reserves and Swiss franc liquidity. This SF/$ swap is a relatively new instrument, having been first used officially in mid July 1977. Depending on the currency and liquidity situation these SF/$ swaps can have a maturity of anywhere between one week and three months. The effect on domestic interest rates and the exchange rate is largely dependent on the length of their maturity. So far the SF/$ swaps have been used exclusively to reduce liquidity over the short term. For such swaps of a long term nature their effect could be quite similar to that of a direct export of capital as commercial banks would readjust their portfolios to compensate for the reduced liquidity. At the present time since the National Bank has more than enough dollar reserves it appears doubtful whether Bank officials will be able to make widespread use of the long term or even renewable SF/$ swaps.

Article 8 of the Swiss Banking Law provides the National Bank with several other instruments of control over monetary reserves particularly in regard to capital exports:

1.   National Bank approval is needed for foreign bond or share issues floated in Switzerland.
2.   National Bank authorization is required for bank loans to non-residents if the amount is greater than 1 million Swiss francs and the maturity is greater than 12 months.
3.   National Bank approval is also needed for mutual funds which are interested in investing predominantly in foreign securities.
4.   Finally National Bank approval is needed for the introduction of all new foreign shares on the Swiss stock exchange.

The purpose of these provisions is to regulate important

channels of capital outflow in a way that will support the National Bank's policy objectives. According to the Bank Law: "The National Bank is authorized, in the interest of the National Currency, the development of the interest rates on the money or capital markets, or the economic welfare of the nation, to refuse permission for any of the above transactions (1-4) or to subject their performance to special conditions".

Also under Article 8 of the Banking Act is one of the most important instruments for controlling reserves: the conversion requirement for certain capital exports. According to this requirement commercial banks are obliged to convert up to 100% of the credit or new issue into foreign currency directly at the National Bank. In this way the commercial banks lose cash reserves in the form of balances at the National Bank. These cash reserves can be made good again to the extent that the National Bank buys foreign currency against Swiss francs and credits the equivalent value of these foreign exchange purchases to the commercial banks. The conversion requirement is nowadays one of the most effective instruments to control the monetary base. It is this conversion requirement that goes farthest in compensating for the National Bank's direct intervention on the foreign exchange markets. In 1976 for example, the National Bank made sales on the foreign exchange market of nearly 15.5 billion Swiss francs; its purchases were about 3.5 billion Swiss francs greater. This difference of 3.5 billion Swiss francs corresponds to a decrease in the money supply of about 6%.

In 1978 the tables were turned because of the plunging dollar. The excess of sales over purchases of Swiss francs on the exchange markets corresponded to an amount equal to an increase of nearly 18% in M1. Hence we were not surprised to see a jump of nearly 20% in the monetary base held by the banks. However, the inflationary impact of this increase in the monetary base was quickly mitigated by a number of factors: the National Bank began to sell off excess dollars in 1979, many of the Swiss francs in the banks were held by foreigners who did not, or could not, reinvest the francs in the Swiss economy, and in general, because of low interest rates, the banks kept the Swiss francs with the National Bank in their giro accounts. What at first look appeared to be a volatile situation was quickly stabilized.

The National Bank continues to have a decided preference for basing monetary policy not so much on interest rate fluctuations but rather through direct intervention such as credit ceilings, the regulation and control of capital outflows and capital export requirements. Because Switzerland is so highly exposed to international money movements the National Bank has a choice between trying to dampen exchange rate fluctuations whenever there are international interest rate changes or regulating domestic interest rate changes whenever there are exchange rate fluctuations. The National Bank has openly chosen the former. So long as inflation rates are low in Switzerland as compared to those of its trading partners the National Bank will continue on this course. At present with domestic interest rates stable the National Bank wants to avoid any involvement that might upset this balance.

II. Open Market Policy

The open market portfolio at the National made up of long term bonds of the Federal government and the railways, national debt claims and universal debentures of the cantons. From 1950 to 1971 the average holdings of such open market papers by the National Bank was about 50 million Swiss francs. During the early part of the 70s ('72-'74) there were times when the National Bank had no open market paper at its disposal. Since 1976 however, the National Bank has built up its holdings in its open market portfolio and now has somewhat over 900 million francs worth of such papers.

Open market policy is a well known instrument of monetary policy in the United States. Theoretically its usage is quite clear: to reduce the money supply the central bank sells some of its open market papers; to increase the money supply they do the opposite. Important here, as compared to discount rate and lombard policy, is that the initiative for change in open market policy comes directly from the central bank. As it seems to be such an effective instrument it is therefore surprising that the Swiss National Bank makes little or no use of open market policy. Even with the increase in the open market portfolio in recent years, the National Bank still has done next to nothing to create a market or open market papers. Compared to the volume of transactions made on the foreign exchange market by the National Bank the volume of open market operations is insignificant.

There are a number of reasons why the National Bank does not make use of open market policy and why they probably will continue to make little use of this instrument.

One of the primary factors discouraging open market operations is the Swiss National Bank Law of 1953. Under this law the National Bank is strictly limited as to the amount of open market type papers they can acquire. The problem is that the National Bank is required by Article 39 of this law to have "gold or short term asset" backing for their banknotes. Most of the paper used for open market operations cannot qualify as backing for the banknotes because their maturities are of too long term. To serve as backing for the banknotes the open market papers would have to have maturities of less than two years. The present law makes it legally impossible to build up the volume of open market papers sufficiently so as to make open market policy feasible.

To some extent the National Bank at times can get around this by purchasing the bonds of public companies. Back in 1974 when Switzerland was trying to pull itself out of a recession, Franz Leutwieler, the President of the Swiss National Bank, said "that some of the increase in the money supply we are striving for is being accomplished not through the exchange markets but through the open market purchases of public corporate bonds."[1] Certainly there are possibilities for open market purchases in the public sector but in the law there is not yet the leverage for the National Bank to sell its own bonds.

The National Bank is also hesitant to become actively involved in open market policy for reasons we mentioned in an earlier section. If the National Bank were to begin using open market policy as one of its chief instruments of control it is fearful of the effects this would have on the interest rate structure and in turn the Swiss franc exchange rate. As already mentioned the National Bank prefers whenever possible to influence the monetary base with a minimum effect on interest rates, particularly over the short term. In the first round open market policy by the

National Bank would effect the demand for open market papers and thereby directly lead to a flucutation in interest rates.

If the Bank instead follows a policy of direct currency intervention the first round effect is on the exchange rate and only later will interest rates adjust.

No doubt if the National Bank would one day feel comfortable with an economic model of how open market policy could work to enhance monetary policy, then open market operations might complement currency intervention. At present though, the institutional limitations to establishing a working open market portfolio are quite substantial. Even if there is to be a revision in the National Bank Law it seems doubtful whether open market policy will ever be allowed to function as anything more than a subsidiary instrument of control.

III. Variations in the Reserve Component

Sterilizing Rescriptions of the State

The sterilization rescriptions are to be found on the liabilities side of the National Bank balance sheet. As of January 1979 these rescriptions totalled 3.4 billion Swiss francs. They are medium term bonds issued to commercial banks by the National Bank. The interest paid on the bonds comes directly from the National Bank and is usually kept right in line with other market rates. The maturity of the bonds is anywhere from 6 to 12 months. The sterilization rescriptions are not marketable. In the case of a liquidity crisis, however, they can be retired by the National Bank at the end of each quarter. Should a commercial bank in need of liquidity find itself with a sterilization rescription that has a maturity of less than three months, it can bring the rescription to the National Bank for discounting.

The sterilization rescriptions are used these days by the National Bank to exert pressure on the reserves of commercial banks. When the commercial banks take up sterilization rescriptions in their portfolios they are trading cash (giro) accounts at the National Bank for secondary liquidity. Commercial banks are willing to invest their excess reserves in these bonds, however, because of the interest they can earn. Furthermore, the banks know if they need liquidity they can always discount these rescriptions when they have maturities of less than 3 months. Rather than unilaterally impose higher minimum reserve requirements, the National Bank gives commercial banks the chance to invest their excess reserves with the National Bank and earn interest. Should the commercial banks refuse the sterilization rescriptions at the interest rate offered by the National Bank, the National Bank at the next appropriate occasion may well increase the minimum reserve requirements.

By soaking up some of the excess reserves of the commercial banks through the sterilization rescriptions the National Bank diminishes the extent to which multiple expansion in the money supply can occur. In such a way the sterilization rescriptions are similar to open market paper.

The net effect of fluctuations in the sterilization rescription portfolio of the National Bank is dependent upon the liquidity situation and the maturity of the bonds. In the short run banks that have sterilization rescriptions of long maturities (over 3 months) will proably make readjustments in their portfolio so that their demand for primary liquidity will be increased. This will have a tendency, depending on the liquidity situation, to raise short term interest rates.

Over the longer term, however, the commercial banks can look at their sterilization rescriptions as a manner of excess reserves which earn interest. If liquidity is needed in the long term it is always possible for a commercial bank to discount its sterilization rescriptions at the National Bank.

If the National Bank wants to make the sterilization rescriptions soak up liquidity over the longer term then their maturities must be lengthened. Whether or not commercial banks would then invest in sterilization rescriptions is questionable. Sterilization rescriptions as an instrument of control are basically hard to deal with. The National Bank cannot guess very effectively as to what an increase in their volume will mean for the interest rates and Swiss franc exchange rate. The most effective time to make use of the sterilization rescriptions is during periods of high excess liquidity. It is during these times that banks will find the sterilization rescriptions most attractive. Through the rescriptions the Swiss National Bank can skim off quite a lot of the excess liquidity from the market.

Sterilization through the State's Account at the National Bank

In February of 1976, the National Bank worked closely with the government to sterilize some of the excess liquidity in the economy. As the interest rate began to sink on Swiss capital markets owing to the excess liquidity, the government issued special bonds. The funds provided by these bonds were used to cover the needs of the Treasury for that year. All of the excess funds they acquired were put into their giro account at the National Bank and sterilized (that is, taken out of circulation). Essentially the whole operation worked like an open market purchase except that in this case it was very much of a one time deal.

Minimum Reserves

In Switzerland the minimum reserve policy of the National Bank is very much different from its counterpart in the United States. The reserves a bank is required to hold are fixed by law, and not variable; such reserves have already been discussed in the first section of this book. Because the rules regulating reserves are fixed, it is difficult for the National Bank to make any use of reserves as an instrument of monetary policy.

For many years there have been discussions and plans to give the National Bank more control over the reserves held by banks. Through emergency legislation and gentlemen's agreements the National Bank has had some control over bank reserves, from time to time. In 1955 in a gentlemen's agreement the commercial banks and a number of finance companies agreed to maintain a minimum credit balance at the National Bank. The purpose of the agreement was to quickly sterilize a portion of the excess liquidity. The amount of the balance to be held at the National Bank was a fixed sum and there were no conditions for variation in this balance by the National Bank.

There were other agreements reached with the banks regarding reserves in '71 and '72. In a government decree issued October 8, 1971 minimum reserves for foreign deposits were demanded by the National Bank. In July of 1972 a decree establishing minimum reserves for domestic liabilities also went into effect.

In the new National Bank Law which is still being written in the Swiss Parliament there are substantive plans to give the National Bank much broader powers over the control of bank reserves. Article 16(a) in the planned revision gives the National Bank the right to increase minimum reserves of commercial banks as a part of their monetary policy.[2] In the revised Bank Law the minimum reserve will reflect the condition and growth of bank deposits as well as the growth of bank loans. In other words, the National Bank will demand minimum reserves on both sides of the balance sheet. The reserve requirements on the assets side will give the National Bank particularly strong control over credit growth in Switzerland. As one may imagine, this is very unpopular with most of the commercial banks. They see such reserve powers as detrimental to competition, as "a political tool of interference," an impairment to capital accumulation by the banks, and a precursor to the establishment of a "gray" credit market outside of the traditional financial market.

According to Professor Franz Ritzmann there are other problems to having a reserve requirement on Bank loans in addition to those mentioned above.[3] Most importantly he points to the fact that although the importance of reserve requirements is that they should help the National Bank control the money supply, reserve requirements on bank loans in Switzerland will not do this. Swiss banks get most of their excess liquidity not from domestic credit expansion but rather from the sale of foreign currencies. Having minimum reserves on domestic credit will do little to effect this money creation. Professor Ritzmann agrees with the banks that such minimum reserve requirements should not be allowed. Certainly if the new National Bank Law is to be passed there will have to be some revision of this section if it is to appeal to its constituency.

Having considered what the new National Bank Law aims to do with minimum reserve requirements let us now turn back to the government decrees of 1971 and 1972 and see how they have effected National Bank monetary policy.

First, we will consider the minimum reserves and negative interest rates on foreign deposits. Such policy is directed at reducing the amount of foreign capital flowing into Switzerland. Since minimum reserves on foreign deposits are generally higher than those on domestic deposits, banks are discouraged from accepting foreign over domestic deposits. The negative interest rates are meant as a strong deterrent to foreigners keeping their funds in Switzerland, but with the Swiss franc appreciating as rapidly as it has the effectiveness of these negative interest rates is dubious at best. Furthermore, as Professor Ritzmann notes in his book, the connection between reserves on foreign deposits and in turn their effect on the money supply is quite tenuous. Ritzmann argues that the domestic credit structure is quite unaffected by changes in minimum reserve requirements for foreign deposits. The foreign assets of the Swiss banks have always been sufficient to cover their foreign liabilities. In other words he postulates that the banks are either reinvesting this money abroad or simply letting it sit; and this can then, in no way, effect the domestic money supply.

Minimum reserves on domestic liabilities, however, certainly do have a direct effect on the money supply. Raising the reserve requirements on demand deposits reduces the money multiplier and therefore the money supply M_1. Reserve requirements on time and savings deposits, though, have less of a direct effect on the money supply. Changing reserve requirements on time and savings deposits should lead banks to make shifts in the structure of their liabilities. This, however, takes time and is influenced by other factors that are usually beyond the control of the National Bank.

Other Controls on Credit

In December of 1975 the Federal decree governing the control of commercial bank credit was extended for another three years. From the power granted to it by the Federal Government the National Bank is able to control the growth rate of domestic bank credit. The commercial banks are permitted to maintain a certain level of credit growth. If they exceed this level of growth they must place an amount equal to the amount by which they exceeded their credit limitation into a blocked account at the

National Bank for a period of at least three months. The National Bank is given discretionary power to demand these funds whenever they feel the credit conditions warrant it.

Under Article 10 of the Banking Act banks with assets of over 20 million Swiss francs are required to give the National Bank advance notice of any planned reduction in maturities or increase in interest rates for medium term notes. The reason for this is that the medium term notes are a very important source of refinancing for mortgages. In Switzerland where the mortgage debt per capita is highest in the world, mortgage rates are quick to adapt to interest rate changes. The National Bank therefore carefully examines all proposals for interest rate changes in light of their repercussions on the money and capital markets. The National Bank can then advise the commercial bank as to whether the proposed change should be postponed, cancelled or modified.

Another reason for keeping interest rates at a low level is that whenever interest rates rise in Switzerland there is considerable capital inflow as foreign funds are attracted by the higher interest rates. This again can lead to exchange rate fluctuations, a situation which the Swiss National Bank is eager to minimize.

IV. Refinancing

The demand for refinancing by commercial banks is largely dependent on their reserve positions. The National Bank, then, can affect the amount of refinancing done by the banks either through its minimum reserve and credit requirements or by the way it provides the banks with financing. The methods of refinancing practiced by the National Bank will be considered below.

Discount and Lombard Policy

The National Bank Act gives the National Bank the power to discount bills and make lombard advances.* As instruments of control, however, discount and lombard policy is quite ineffective. In Switzerland the amount of public and private liabilities in the form of bills is small. As a percentage of total bank assets the

*Lombard advances are loans made by the Swiss National Bank against specified securities. See page 98 for further description.

amount of discount and lombard advances comes to under 2%.[4]

TABLE 5. Assets of the Swiss National Bank (11/79)
in millions of francs

Gold Holdings	11,904	34%
Currency	21,353	61%
Foreign Treasury Bills	—	—
Discounts	289	1%
Lombard advances	24	—
Open Market papers	931	3%
Other	250	1%

The high degree of liquidity that historically exists in Switzerland makes discounting as a source of refinancing quite unnecessary. Commercial bank recourse to obtaining National Bank credit is quite small. In fact in regard to discount policy as an instrument of monetary control we can say it is really non-existent. As there is a quantitative limitation on the amount of discountable paper the official discount rate can remain below the market interest rate without having any expansionary effect on the money supply. One would think that this would have encouraged banks to borrow from the National Bank but as the opportunities for this are small and the discounts of such short term (legal limit is three months maturity) the banks have made little use of this discount window subsidy. Self-financing and interbank transfers have proved to be more than adequate means for the banks to refinance themselves when needed.

For 30 years prior to 1957 the official discount rate was fixed at one and one-half percent. Since then, with the exception of 1975, there has been little variation in the official discount rate. As already mentioned the discount rate is certainly not a good indicator of National Bank monetary policy. Take, for example, the period of 1964-1972.There were wide gyrations in the growth of the money supply, yet the discount rate never responded to this. In the graph below, one can see how unresponsive the discount rate has been to fluctuations in the money supply and how poor an indicator it is of monetary policy. The chief role of National Bank discounts in the Swiss banking system has probably been to provide liquidity in the balance sheet for the quarterly closings and now, through the short term swaps, even this use for discounting is diminishing.

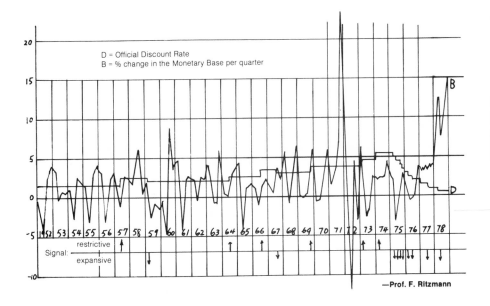

D = Official Discount Rate
B = % change in the Monetary Base per quarter

—Prof. F. Ritzmann

The lombard advances are loans made by the National Bank against federal bonds and other national debt bonds from cantons, communities and the cantonal banks. The bonds of Swiss financial and industrial firms are also permitted as collateral but the advances made against such paper is limitèd and can only be made if certain criteria are met. The National Bank has the right to demand repayment of all such loans after giving 10 days advance notice.

The purpose of the lombard loans is to provide commercial banks with liquidity when they temporarily run low on funds. Lombard credit just like discount credit is not unlimited. Banks have a precisely determined limit of such credits, based on a percentage of their capital, which they are allowed to take. Also like discount credits lombard advances are used most frequently at the end of each financial quarter when liquidity is needed on the banks as "window dressing ."

Short Term $/SF Swaps

Unquestionably the largest amount of refinancing is done through the short term $/SF swap. The way this works is through a swap arrangement set up between commercial banks and the National Bank. The commercial banks obtain Swiss francs by selling foreign currency to the National Bank in fixed amounts. The commercial banks must agree to repurchase these sums within a month.

Short term swaps account for about two-thirds of the money made available by the National Bank to cover end of the month and end of the year liquidity demand. The banks eagerly make use of this method of refinancing as it is low in cost, readily accessible, and available in large amounts. The National Bank, for its part, is eager to engage in the swaps in order to avoid end of month fluctuations in the Swiss franc exchange rate. If it were not for the short term $/SF swaps the commercial banks would have to go to the open market for their Swiss franc liquidity needs periodically and thereby temporarily inflate the Swiss franc exchange rate.

Around the time of their quarterly statements the banks liquidity requirements are quite large and the National Bank meets this temporary need by providing the banks with short

TABLE 6

Refinancing Help from the Swiss National Bank
(in billions of Swiss francs)

Balance at end of month

	Discount and Lombard credits		Sterilizing Rescriptions		Dollar-SF Swaps		Total Refinancing Help	
	1978	1977	1978	1977	1978	1977	1978	1977
January	0.30	0.93	—	0.67	0.29	0.30	0.59	1.90
February	0.26	1.34	—	0.67	0.29	1.10	0.55	3.11
March	1.22	1.95	1.53	0.75	0.10	3.15	2.85	5.85
April	0.70	2.00	—	0.67	—	0.57	0.71	3.24
May	1.96	2.00	0.24	0.13	—	1.29	2.20	3.42
June	1.74	2.20	2.17	0.68	2.52	3.18	6.44	6.06
July	1.92	1.51	—	0.20	0.80	0.51	2.73	2.22
August	1.01	1.55	—	0.20	2.78	0.24	3.80	1.99
September	0.92	1.93	1.40	0.80	4.27	1.10	6.58	3.83
October	0.25	1.21	—	0.20	2.52	—	2.77	1.41
November	0.25	1.71	0.01	0.20	2.52	0.66	2.78	2.57
December	0.29	1.72	0.51	1.12	2.52	2.51	3.32	5.35

—SNB Annual Report (1978)

term stand-by credit and, as we have already discussed in a previous section, the discounting and refinancing of sterilization rescriptions. The time periods for which the National Bank grants credit through these various instruments is exclusively over the short term. The effect upon interest rates and the exchange rate therefore is quite minimal.

There may, however, be a noticeable effect upon the money supply, that in turn could later come to affect interest rates. An increase in the demand for refinancing credits will cause an increase in the money multipler as the demand for cash holdings go up. Usually, though, such changes in the demand for refinancing credit are only temporary and the money supply too slow to react to such short term fluctuations.

The instruments of financing are effective means of controlling short term liquidity. Commercial banks make frequent use of refinancing at the National Bank for "window dressing" on their balance sheets (see chart above). Which type of refinancing method the commercial banks use is dependent upon a number of factors, most important being the relative interest costs of each type of method. The total cost of refinancing, however, must also take into account the opportunity cost of having primary or secondary liquidity. During the sixties, for example, although the interest cost of discounting was below that of the short term $/SF swaps the banks preferred to achieve their liquidity through the swaps. The cost of having to hold discountable paper was seen as greater by the banks than the relative interest cost differential between discounting and short term $/SF swaps.

The variety of instruments of control that can be utilized by the Swiss National Bank is quite extensive. For the most part these instruments are used sparingly as National Bank Law and the constitution prohibits intensive interference by the National Bank. Where possible direct intervention through credit ceilings and regulation of capital flows is the preferred means of control. Changes in the foreign exchange holdings of the National Bank are probably the most often used and effective of the instruments available. This is not only because of their direct connection to the monetary base but also because their effect on interest rates and the exchange rate is easiest to anticipate.

The Swiss Capital Controls of 1978

To make capital inflows into Switzerland more difficult the Swiss authorities passed several new sets of regulations on February 24, 27, and on March 1, 1978. These moves were taken by the Swiss government in response to the rapid appreciation of the Swiss franc (over 20%) in the early months of 1978. The Swiss National Bank said the action was necessary "to safeguard the Swiss franc and the National economy". It is their view that the Swiss franc has become overvalued as a result of speculative actions in the foreign exchange markets over the preceding few months. The Swiss National Bank was anxious to curb this appreciation as they feared the effect it could have on their export industry. The Swiss, for example, do not want to see the franc appreciate faster than the currency of its most important trading partner, West Germany. Otherwise they fear their exports to West Germany will no longer remain competitive. It is their feeling that this can be avoided by stopping the massive capital inflows which they see as the cause of the franc's appreciation.

Many of these restrictions from 1978 are no longer in effect but we shall consider them anyhow. They give us an insight into National Bank policy, into the sources of capital inflows and perhaps most importantly these measures give us an indication of what to expect should the National Bank act again in the future to to curb capital inflows.

The measures that were taken by the Swiss authorities can be summarized as follows:

1. There was a reduction made in the National Bank's lending rate to financial institutions from 1.5 to 1%. This was directed at reducing the interest paid on Swiss franc deposits.
2. No non-resident could make any new purchases in Switzerland of stocks issued by Swiss companies. (This was lifted in early 1979). It was also forbidden to export securities, that are traded in Switzerland, for the purpose of selling them to foreigners. Non-residents, however, could purchase stocks issued by non-Swiss companies that are traded in Swiss francs in Switzerland. Non-residents may keep any stocks of Swiss companies they already own.
3. No non-resident may make any new purchases in Switzerland of existing bonds denominated in Swiss francs. This applies both to bonds issued by the Swiss and by foreign entities. As with stocks present holdings may be kept. For future issues of Swiss franc bonds 35% can be sold to non-residents.
4. The negative interest tax rulings remain as when they were first established in 1974. Any non-resident who had a Swiss bank account on October 31, 1974 may hold up to 100,000 Swiss francs above his October 1974 balance. Of this amount he may have in an interest bearing account up to 20,000 Swiss francs above his October 1974 interest bearing balance. Non-residents who did not have Swiss bank accounts on October 31, 1974 may keep up to 100,000 Swiss francs in a Swiss bank account, and of this amount 20,000 Swiss francs may draw interest. (amended, see ch. 20)

    Note: These regulations apply to each bank account on an individual. So the limits here may be exceeded by having an account at more than one bank. Also note that these restrictions do not apply to accounts in currencies other than Swiss francs.
5. The importation of foreign banknotes is limited to the equivalent of 20,000 Swiss francs per person in any three months period (Cancelled).

6. Any non-resident whose bank balance exceeds 1 million Swiss francs must take a one time reduction of 20% of the amount in excess of 1 million Swiss francs. For example, an account with 2 million Swiss francs must be reduced by 200,000 Swiss francs (This was as of April 1, 1978).

7. Also as of April 1, 1978 a 10% negative interest charge per quarter was levied on all bank accounts of non-residents who had over 5 million in Swiss francs (about 3 million dollars). (See ch. 20)

8. Foreign central banks have become subject to the same negative interest rate mentioned above. If they have any Swiss franc accounts in Swiss banks in excess of 5 million Swiss francs they will be charged negative 10% on that amount per quarter. This requirement was meant to discourage central banks from using the Swiss franc as a reserve currency. (see ch. 20)

9. Purchases of Swiss francs through forward contracts are now limited. For contracts maturing in 10 days or less, a bank may hold contracts with a total value of no more than 20% of the value of such contracts held on October 31, 1974. For a contract with more than 10 days maturity the limit is 50%. Note these limits only apply to long positions in the Swiss franc and are only for contracts of the bank's customers. For contracts held for its own account the bank is not limited here.

10. The net foreign currency position of each bank, however, must be long every day. In other words at the end of each business day the bank is required to be short the Swiss franc.

How effective have all these measures been in reducing the appreciation of the Swiss franc? Not very, as the Swiss franc has continued to appreciate in the period since these controls and disincentives were first introduced. Apparently the Swiss are not having much success in stemming the tide of massive capital inflows.

Let us now examine this issue of capital inflows more carefully to determine why these capital controls have been so ineffective. In an article entitled, "The Case Against Capital Controls for Balance of Payments Reasons," Gottfried Haberler took a close look at the whole problem of capital inflows. He distinguished between three types of capital flows in the international system. There were those flows induced by interest differentials, those induced by the expectation of parity changes and those induced by primarily political factors, "such as fear of war, revolution, political and racial persecution and confiscation or appropriation."[4] We will now examine how effective the Swiss measures were within the framework of these capital flows.

The lowering of the lending rate by the National Bank from 1.5 to 1% was obviously aimed at discouraging the capital flows resulting from category one. The interest rate is so low already, however, that a change has little effect on discouraging inflows. When one is practically at zero to begin with any reduction becomes an exercise in futility as one finds oneself lacking the needed leverage. Central bankers are used to seeing interest rates as indicators of the price of money domestically but they often fail to realize that the same relationship does not exist in the international arena. These days interest rates reflect inflation rates. So the lower the inflation rate, the lower the interest rate and the more attractive the currency becomes. So long as the interest rate continues to reflect the low rates of inflation in Switzerland then the attitude towards the Swiss franc as an inflation hedge will remain bullish.

The second category: Capital flows induced by the expectation of parity changes unquestionably is the most important reaason behind the massive capital inflows into Switzerland. Psychology, these days, may be nearly as important as balance of payment considerations in determining speculative activity on the foreign exchange markets. Switzerland after a century old tradition of peace, freedom and political and economic stability has managed to gain the trust of international investors. People have come to believe in the stability of the Swiss economic scene and this has had a reinforcing effect on their economy. It is also important to remember that as confidence in the dollar erodes the Swiss franc becomes more and more attractive an alternative investment or reserve currency. Remember that the stock of international dollars has become so huge in relation to the supply of alternative reserve assets (particularly the Swiss franc) that just a tiny move out of dollars can create large currency price movements.

Consider, for example, the demand pressure on the Swiss franc if only 5% of the Euro dollars held were switched into Swiss francs. This amount of nearly 65 billion Swiss francs would represent a sum almost equal to the entire national income of Switzerland.

The reasons for speculative capital to move into Switzerland, during this age of uncertainty on foreign exchange markets, are quite numerous. In terms of straight economics we can point to the growing U.S. trade deficit, the lack of a comprehensive energy program and periodically political and economic unrest of a comprehensive energy program and periodically political and economic unrest in the U.S. (Energy crises, Carter's low popularity, inflation) that detract from the dollar's image as an international currency. Switzerland, on the other hand, has been running steady balance of payment surpluses; strikes are a nearly unknown phenomena and politically the Swiss have been able to preserve their neutrality.

Political neutrality is an important element in the massive capital inflows that come from France and Italy. In recent years as the prospect for a communist or socialist victory in these governments has grown, people have tried to transfer their wealth to Switzerland despite the restrictions on capital outflows in their own country.

The Swiss controls prohibiting the purchase of Swiss securities, the import of large amounts of currency and the negative interest rates on Swiss franc accounts are all aimed at reducing these capital flows. But there were enough loopholes and problems with their enforcement so as to limit their effectiveness. Recognizing the inefficiencies of these restrictions, the National Bank began to lift some of them in late 1978 and 1979.

As already mentioned, one way around the controls is for the foreigner to maintain accounts at more than one bank as these rules only apply to accounts at each bank. Also under these rules there was no limitations imposed on foreign commercial banks that maintain Swiss franc deposits in Switzerland. It is therefore possible for a foreigner to circumvent Swiss restrictions by having a foreign bank act for him in their name. There are other loopholes; while non-residents may not take additional purchases of older Swiss franc bonds, they are, remember, eligible to buy a portion of new bonds if they are available. Regarding stocks, although those of Swiss companies could not be bought, non-residents were able to buy stocks of non-Swiss companies denominated in Swiss francs and traded in Switzerland.

Probably the biggest loophole of all is through the Euro-Swiss franc market. Investors still keep pressure on the Swiss franc by shifting their Swiss franc holdings to another European country, say Austria. There, not only can they hold unlimited amounts of Swiss francs,but they can also earn interest on their funds. Rumor has it that several central banks tried to maintain their holdings in Swiss francs by shifting them to foreign branches of Swiss banks. The National Bank is considering means to prevent the switching of domestic accounts into the Euro Market accounts.

In terms of enforcement the high administrative costs of supervising these restrictions sometimes make them untenable. Prohibition of physical banknote importation, for example, cannot be effective in a country that has nearly no customs inspection. As a matter of fact, while it was prohibited the amount of banknote importation is thought to have increased. Since people see the Swiss franc as a refuge currency making it more difficult to hold only makes it more attractive psychologically. It was also possible for foreigners to buy the Swiss franc banknotes they wanted abroad and then keep them, for example, in a safe deposit box in New York. We know something like this has probably been occurring as there has been an increasing demand for large denomination Swiss franc notes in the international foreign exchange markets. Judging from past experience such an import limit will never be effective. The Swiss imposed a similar limit in 1976 but lifted it after one hour. This time the restrictions lasted several months, but National Bank officials still do not discount their use again in the future.

Considerable problems also arise when trying to enforce these controls without causing a great degree of disruption in the domestic economy. The Swiss restrictions on security and bond purchases, for example, had a depressing effect on their market value. By keeping a group of investors out of the stock and bond markets the government has effectively lowered the demand curve for these assets. Additionally, the imposition of restrictions measures on the purchase of Swiss securities has historically resulted in a black arbitrage between Switzerland and Germany.

This is possible because of the lack of detailed customs inspection and banking secrecy.

Also if we remember the lowering of the domestic bank lending rate we can see that it will have some effects on the domestic economy as well. The lowered rate will have the effect of stimulating domestic investment. This is beneficial in so far as it offsets the recessionary effect of the loss in exports due to the high exchange rates. Unfortunately though, it will cause a general stimulation of the economy rather than a specific relief for the hard hit export industries.

Looking back on these controls, their costs (both administrative and economic) and their implications, we have seen that they are not nearly as effective as the Swiss National Bank would have hoped them to be. Controls alone are never going to stop the appreciation of the Swiss franc, at best all they can do is slow it down. Other countries have tried implementing controls against capital inflows in the past and their success has been very limited. The Swiss will find, like the monetary authorities in France did in 1973, that many people will be willing to break laws and able to find loopholes if there are prospects for large profits.

The Swiss have done everything that is possible to dissuade interest in the franc except the one thing that would in fact work, that is engage in activity in the market on a continuous basis to effect a parity with the Deutsche mark and the U.S. Dollar. They have avoided this tack because they have not wanted to inflate their money supply. It is doubtful whether they will loosen this tight grip on the rate of monetary growth as they are interested in keeping inflation at very low levels.

Recently the National Bank stated that it was indirectly participating in the European Monetary System by agreeing to link the Swiss franc with the Deutsche mark. At first look many thought this would be inflationary for the Swiss as the Deutsche mark is the main supporting currency in the EMS, but the fears of inflation in Switzerland from this source are unfounded. The Deutsche mark continues to be a strong currency and the rate of inflation in Switzerland is still far below that of other countries. The bottom is not falling out beneath the European Monetary System but rather from beneath the dollar. At present the EMS needs little support and so long as the Swiss are able to keep their inflation rate below that experienced by the U.S. and Germany the demand for the Swiss franc will continue whether or not they are participating in the EMS and whether or not there are capital controls.

CHAPTER 12

The Swiss Franc and Monetary Policy

When considering why the Swiss franc is such a strong currency probably the best place to begin our study is with a consideration of how the Swiss have managed to keep their rate of inflation so low. In 1979 their rate of inflation was 4.2% and in 1980 it is expected to be around 3%. Price stability in Switzerland, however, has not always been the case; during the 1963-1973 period, inflation in Switzerland was not better than the OECD average of 4.6%. As recently as 1974 Swiss prices jumped 9.8%.

Judging from these statistics we must conclude that somehow over the past few years the Swiss have found some means of combatting inflation. We become even more impressed when we also consider the fact that the Swiss economy has remained relatively stable and that unemployment has remained nearly negligible despite the rapid decrease in inflation:

TABLE 7
UNEMPLOYMENT

	75	76	77	78*
Real GNP (in million Swiss francs)	97.610	139.9	140.7	141.3
Unemployment (as a percent of total working force)	.9%	.6%	.5%	.5%

*1978 estimates　　　　　　　　　　—Source OECD surveys

From what we know of elementary economics we would have suspected the large drop in the inflation rate (from 7.4% to 1.4%) to produce considerable ramifications for the economy in terms of a higher level of unemployment and a reduced rate of growth. In the U.S., the past three administrations have been hesitant to cut back on the growth of the money supply as they feared the repercussions this would have on credit conditions and unemployment. Well, Switzerland has no magic formula for curing

Trend of prices   Percentage change from previous year

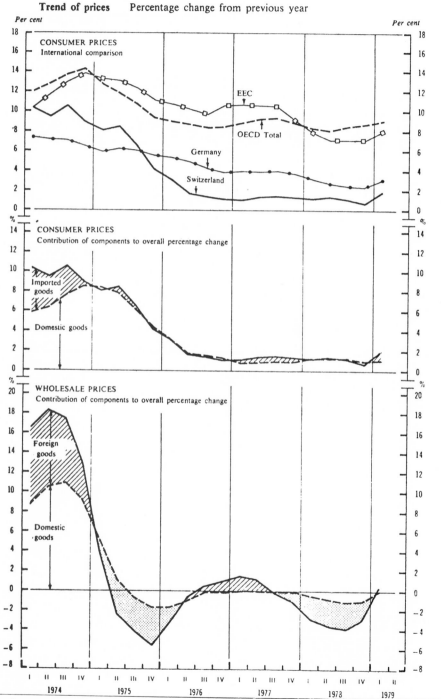

Sources: OECD. Main Economic Indicators; Swiss National Bank. Monthly Bulletin; Swiss Submission to OECD.

Development of Consumer and Wholesale Prices in Switzerland

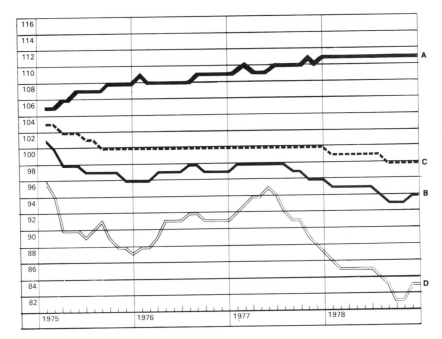

A Consumer price index   Index: 1974 average = 100
B Wholesale price index
C Wholesale price index for domestic goods
D Wholesale price index for imported goods

—**SNB annual report 1978**

inflation; the Swiss, too, had to pull in their belts while fighting inflation. They managed to fight inflation so effectively only because of a number of unique circumstances which happened to be working in their favor at the time. In the next few pages we will consider what these conditions were and what the implications of these conditions are for the future.

The most important step taken by the Swiss in combatting inflation was to follow a tight monetary policy in the years 1972 to 1974. If we look at the percentage growth in M_1 (Notes in circulation and sight deposits) as compared to the rates of inflation over the same period we see an interesting correlation. There appears to be about an 18-24 month lag between changes in the rate of growth of the money supply and changes in the rate of inflation. In 1971, for example, the money supply (M_1) grew at a whopping 21% over the previous year; by the middle of 1973 prices suddenly began to rise quickly from 8% to 12%. In 1972 the Swiss began to tighten their monetary policy. The rate of increase in the money supply was 8.5, 2.0 and 1.1% respectively for the years 1972 to 1974. Inflation during this period went from a high of 12% at the end of 1972 to a low of 3.6% at the end of 1975.

The economy, however, was not left unaffected by the severe cutback in the money supply. Beginning in 1973 the GNP of Switzerland in real terms began to sink and by 1975 Switzerland was thrown into recession. The real gross national product dropped 7.6% in 1975. This was the most severe recession suffered by any of the OECD countries at this time.

The U.S. drop in real GNP for the same period was only 1.8% and the whole OECD area averaged only a 1% drop in real GNP. For Switzerland this was the largest drop in GNP ever recorded. In the first half of 1975 the seasonally adjusted index of industrial production dropped at an annual rate of more than 27%. Household private consumption fell by about 2.5%. Output of plant and machinery decreased by about 15%. Foreign demand for Swiss exports was also severely down due to the worldwide recession; exports of goods and services were down about 7% for the year. This is quite important when one remembers that exports represent roughly 33% of Switzerland's GNP on the average. Unemployment also went up sharply during this period, but we

Development of Swiss Gross National Product 1972-1979

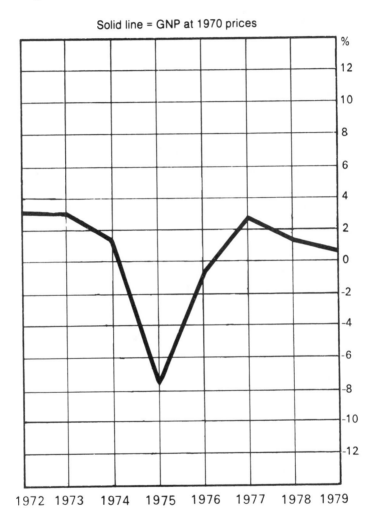

Solid line = GNP at 1970 prices

will have more to say about this later.

First we must consider why the Swiss National Bank tightened up their monetary policy so quickly and efficiently. We must remember that the advent of floating exchange rates during this period was to play a major role in redirecting National Bank monetary policy.

Before the Swiss franc was allowed to float in August 1971 Switzerland's inflationary troubles were being imported from abroad. Switzerland was particularly vulnerable to imported inflation because of a) the relatively large size of its foreign trade sector (35% of GNP) and b) the importance of Switzerland as an international financial center. Inflation abroad was channelled into these two sectors by a)price effects, b) demand effects and c) liquidity effects.[1]

Foreign trade prices affect domestic inflation in several ways. First, since Switzerland is heavily dependent on her trading partners for raw material there is considerable domestic impact from an increase in import prices. Second, higher import prices for raw materials raise production costs in Switzerland. In 1973, for example, there was a large increase in the price of oil. This led to a 51.4% increase in the amount of Swiss francs spent for lubricants and fuel over the previous year. This increase was passed on to the consumer in terms of higher energy costs, higher prices for finished products and greater demand for domestic substitutes (e.g. more hydroelectric power).

Under the fixed exchange rate system perhaps the most important source of inflationary pressure came from the massive inflows of funds from abroad due to exchange rate speculation. In 1971, for example, there was a net inflow of 2.4 billion. Demand for Swiss francs was so high that the National Bank was obliged to make purchases of over 8 billion in one month alone. This had a tremendous effect on increasing the money supply. As the National Bank bought up these currencies, they put more and more Swiss francs into circulation. The amount of foreign currency reserves at the National Bank increased from 4 billion Swiss francs in 1970 to 10.5 billion at the end of 1971; the money supply increased 40.1% in this year.

To combat the capital inflows and their effect the National Bank utilized a number of capital and exchange control policies.

In a Gentlemen's Agreement (that went back to September of 1960), the National Bank along with the commercial banks decided to restrict credit extension for domestic use. They agreed only to allow an increase in mortgage loans (.7% over the previous year) and loans to public authorities (2% above the previous year's total). In another agreement aimed at reducing the excess reserves of commercial banks the National Bank imposed a 200 percent reserve requirement on the net increase in bank foreign liabilities. Additionally in 1972 a 20% reserve requirement was imposed on all increases in domestic demand deposits. The National Bank also adapted a number of direct measures to stop the large foreign inflows. In February of 1972 commercial banks were requested to convert into U.S. dollars at the National Bank (at a fixed rate) 25% of their capaital exports denominated in Swiss francs. The remainder was to be converted into foreign currency at Swiss banks. Later that year the acquisition of Swiss capital assets by foreigners was banned, and a negative interest rate of 5% per annum imposed on foreigners who increased their Swiss franc deposits. These measures in conjunction with the earlier ones helped to slow down the capital inflows and put a brake on credit expansion. During the first nine months of 1972, total domestic credit rose 6.7% compared with 8.7% in 1971, and commercial bank reserves held at the National Bank fell from 12.3 billion Swiss francs in August 1971 to 6.4 billion in December 1972.

The floating exchange rates, as we already mentioned, marked a turning point for National Bank monetary policy. At first the National Bank tried to maintain a passive role with little intervention, but they were soon to see that would not be possible for long. In response to floating rates international portfolio adjustments led to an appreciation of the Swiss franc. Foreigners wanted to place their funds in Switzerland both for investment purposes and for security. The expectations of foreigners pushed up the demand for Swiss francs and as the National Bank was no longer willing to supply more Swiss francs, the Swiss franc had to appreciate vis-à-vis other currencies. The effects of this appreciation are two-fold on the Swiss economy. Most importantly an appreciation of the Swiss franc means that imports become cheaper in relative terms. If we use the example of oil again we find that the percentage increase in prices was 50% in 1973, 30% in 1974 and -8% in 1975. In general, the appreciation of the Swiss franc has helped to contain the use in import prices, and although it has been a handicap to exporters there have been several factors helping to limit these negative effects. With import prices going down in relative terms terms many of the raw materials needed for Swiss industry become 'cheaper,' thereby alleviating some of the inflationary pressures. In other words, just as we would have expected theoretically, the advent of floating exchange rates has made it more difficult to export inflation to Switzerland. As the Swiss franc appreciates imports become more attractive and the demand for domestic substitutes goes down. In Switzerland where so many raw materials come from abroad an appreciating Swiss franc also means that goods at home can be produced more cheaply.

Since 1971 the trend for the Swiss franc has been strongly upward. Compared to a basket of the 15 most important currencies the Swiss franc has appreciated 108% between 1971 and January 1979. One would think that an effect of this would have been an inflationary impact on export prices. A foreign customer would still be paying the same in Swiss francs for Swiss products, and should be finding that he must pay out more and more of his own currency as the Swiss franc appreciates. Any increase in Swiss franc prices would compound this effect. One would expect then that the over 100% appreciation of the Swiss franc has led to a severe reduction in the volume of exports. This is, however, not so.

TABLE NO. 7
SWISS EXPORTS

	'70	'71	'72	'73	'74	'75	'76	'77	'78
Export (in billion francs)	22.1	23.6	26.2	29.9	35.3	33.4	37.0	42.1	41.8

— Source Swiss National Bank

Obviously then our picture of how the appreciation of the Swiss franc is affecting export prices must be somehow faulty. The true competitive situation is, in fact, somewhat more complicated than explained above. Over the past few years other countries' export prices have gone up considerably faster in their own currencies than have the Swiss franc prices of Swiss products. This inflation differential compensates partially for the higher Swiss franc export prices added by the exchange rate. To obtain a more revealing picture of how Swiss export prices compete relative to foreign exports on the international market, one can calculate a trade-weighted appreciation of the Swiss franc. Recently such a weighted appreciation was calculated by economists at the Swiss Bank Corporation. Their findings are quite interesting. In real (trade-weighted) terms they found that the Swiss franc appreciated at an annual rate of 3.6% for 1971-1976 (rather than the nominal rate of 9%). In other words over this period Switzerland's competitive position worsened by an average of 3.6% a year. This must be weighed against the behavior of other Swiss price indexes for the same period. Import prices rose 3% a year an average for the period 1970-1975 but since 1975 import prices and the wholesale price of imported goods went down. The consequence of all this is that the greater the Swiss content of a given product in terms of cost or value added in production, the less steep the price increases. This is an encouraging fact for the Swiss export industry, in the long run, as it is heavily reliant on the value added through production. The appreciation of the currency may place the export industries at a temporary disadvantage in its sales efforts but as cost effects work their way into the industry prices can evolve to further benefit the export sector. If we look at the index of Swiss export prices in recent years we see that there has been little change despite appreciation.

TABLE NO. 8
Swiss Export Prices
Index Basis 1970=100

1974	1975	1976	1977	1978
127	130	130	131	128

From such information on the Swiss franc coupled with the fact that people see Switzerland as a secure refuge for foreign funds, we can expect the appreciation of the Swiss franc to continue. There is still a very large demand for Swiss francs despite capital controls. As the dollar depreciates many individuals and business firms will switch a portion of their investment portfolios into Swiss francs to guard against depreciation losses.

The chief reason for this is, of course, because of the low level of inflation in Switzerland. The purchasing power of the Swiss franc has remained constant or above that of the other major currencies. People's expectations are that this will continue so long as the Swiss are able to maintain low rates of inflation. With the inflation rate for Switzerland having been so low for the last few years demand for the Swiss franc has been high and appreciation always immanent.

We have considered to this point the means by which inflation was combatted in Switzerland. A mixture of floating exchange rates, an appreciating franc, a severe cut in the money supply along with capital and exchange controls all made it possible for Switzerland to reduce its inflation rate by cutting back on credit and going into a recession. We must now consider another aspect of this fight against inflation; namely, how it was possible for Switzerland to accept the repercussion of recession so readily. Although nearly all central bankers agree that tight monetary policy is the answer to inflation, few, if any, can openly take such a step without committing political suicide. In Switzerland, though, circumstances in the early 1970s worked to mitigate the political backlash of pursuing a tight monetary policy.

The severe recession in 1975 was "politically acceptable" because it answered two of the biggest problems confronting the Swiss populace at this time: The concern over high prices and the high level of foreigners working in Switzerland. As the economy took a nose dive these problems began to resolve themselves. Below we examine the reasons for this.

Unemployment soared during the recession. Over the fifteen month period from September 1974 to December 1975 the number of unemployed went from 92 to 26,258. In September of 1974 there were more than 12 job vacancies for every seeker and in December 1975 there were more than 20 job applications for every vacancy. Horrible as these statistics sound, they are only the tip of the iceberg. One source at the Swiss National Bank stated that he estimates that nearly 400,000 jobs were lost during the recession. This represents 15% of the total labor force. He adds, however, that over a quarter of this amount represents those who under ordinary circumstances would have been pensioned or retired. In other words before the recession, Switzerland had more than full employment. He also estimated that 200,000 to 250,000 of the 400,000 unemployed were represented by foreign workers. Most of these, some 200,000 (5-6% of the whole labor force) were sent out of the country. Therefore, a large number of the unemployed never even made it into the statistics. For all practical purposes Switzerland was able to export unemployment during this period. A bill was passed, through a national referendum, that limited the amount of foreign workers allowed into the country. Before the recession it would have been difficult to lower the number of foreign workers in Switzerland. The recession provided a method by which foreign workers could be drawn out of the work force through economic rather than political means.

Another reaction to the recession, and a corollary of the increased unemployment was a slowdown in wage rate increases. With the deterioration of the labor market the rate of increase in hourly wages in industry, which had been more than 10% during 1974, was reduced to less than 7% in 1975 and fell all the way to 1.9% in 1978. Unions all but abandoned new demands in the face of the recession. Strikes, as usual for Switzerland, were virtually non-existent. The appreciation of the Swiss franc did the most to get prices down quickly. As imports got cheaper it became easier for unions to slacken their demands. Although in nominal terms the growth of wage payments slowed down considerably, in real terms the wage earnings of workers went up slightly both in 1977 and 1978.

In the labor market another factor which reflected the Swiss mentality was the willingness of several workers' groups to forego wage increases in order to make themselves more internationally competitive. The hotel industry is a good example. The appreciating Swiss franc has made it more expensive for foreigners to vacation in Switzerland. Tourism is one of the biggest businesses in Switzerland and one might have expected the appreciation of the franc to have a very detrimental effect. In fact though this trend has had comparatively little effect on the industry. One reason for this is because hoteliers have been keeping their costs down by not approving any wage hikes. In their annual meeting at the end of 1977, for example, the union of hotel workers agreed not to press for any wage increases during the year 1978.

Being able to maintain low wage rates and a low level of unemployment was not only politically and economically feasible in the early 1970s but has also led to what has been described as the "virtuous circle." As Switzerland has been able to maintain a low rate of inflation with a minimum of political and economic upheaval, the Swiss franc has become a very desirable asset in investors portfolios. This, as already explained, has led to its appreciation. The appreciation of the Swiss franc has in turn, as we saw above, kept down the cost of imports and thus relieved a large portion of the inflationary pressures on the economy.

We have now examined the chief reasons why the Swiss were able to drastically cut their inflation rate and how they did it. But the reader should not be unduly impressed for they did not escape unscathed. The economy in Switzerland, although it is doing well, is certainly not booming. The construction business hardest hit during the recession still has not recovered. And although prices are not rising they are high to begin with, especially real estate.

It is doubtful whether Switzerland will be able to maintain such low rates of inflation indefinitely. As the economy continues to pick up there will be increased pressure to expand profit margins and wages. There will also be the temptation to increase the rate of growth in the money supply to pick up some of the slack in the economy. Prices will gradually rise in response to the increased demand that would come from an expansionary policy. But to counter these inflationary tendencies the Swiss have several factors which may reduce their effects.

First, the low interest rates in Switzerland in so far as they are a cost factor to industry help to keep inflation in check. Secondly, the Federal Budget is in quite good shape. There is a deficit of some 17 billion Swiss francs but this is only 1.2% of the GNP. As long as the budget is more or less balanced there will be little inflationary pressure from inflationary finance.

Thirdly, the appreciable easing in the labor market at the end of 1974 had a favorable impact on labor productivity in the period since then. Additionally, although employment had fallen by about 11% in two years, unemployment still remained nearly negligible (.9% at its peak). This gave the monetary authorities ample room to manoeuvre as they did not have the political stigma of unemployment to deal with. Finally, we can also say that the difficulties encountered during the recession on the whole helped to strengthen the cooperation between labor and management as they both found themselves working for a common goal.

All of these factors, many of which are unique to Switzerland, had some influence in making a success of that country's policy for fighting inflation. Switzerland's experience with inflation can only serve as a model for other countries to a degree. Other countries may share some of the same conditions that made possible the Swiss success against inflation, but none seem to have the same combination of circumstances to make it both an economic and political actuality. For most nations, because of their size, it would be highly dangerous to try the same path as the Swiss to price stability. If we look at the United States here as a case in point we see that it too shares many of the conditions inherent in the Swiss economy; the U.S. dollar is, despite its recent troubles, basically a desirable currency. Americans have a work ethic and business ability equal to the Swiss and the labor unions in the U.S. are, in general, quite level-headed. The U.S., however, could never engineer a recession like the Swiss. Politically it would be murderous. Unemployment would soar above 12%, and what would the U.S. do? Export workers to Mexico and Canada? No, this would be highly unlikely. Furthermore, if the U.S. went into a deep recession they would initiate self-reinforcing repercussions throughout the world. The same applies to Western Germany except that in their case the ramifications of a severe slump would be confined more to Europe.

Switzerland has done well in its fight against inflation and there are many lessons that can be learned. The Swiss have been both conservative and diligent in their policies. As a result, the Swiss experience with inflation has attracted investors from all over the world.

PART III

HOW
TO USE
SWISS BANKS

CHAPTER 13

The Practical Aspects

A. Why a Swiss Bank Account?

A Swiss bank account is definitely not for everyone. There are a lot of headaches that go along with having an account in Switzerland. Communication with your banker is not always easy, it may be difficult to develop a good rapport with your banker, you will occasionally be confused as to what course he is taking and your government the whole time will be trying to dissuade you from holding any foreign accounts.

If you have a certain outlook on the world, however, these headaches may be worth putting up with. If you are worried about inflation getting out of control, if you think your government has a built in tendency to increasingly interfere in your financial affairs and if you think you should have some privacy over your investments whether for tax or personal reasons then a Swiss account may be for you.

Switzerland is a financial haven just as it is a political one. It owes its existence to this and it is in the best interests of the Swiss, and many governments who transact business there, to preserve Switzerland as it is. In terms of stability Switzerland has few equals either politically or economically.

No one needs to be reminded of the situation faced by German Jews in the 30's. If they had enough money and were lucky they could flee the country before the real trouble began. Others were not as quick to recognize the implications of the Hitler Reich and perhaps did not want to have to leave behind all that they had worked for. Few of those people were able to survive. Only the pessimistic and far sighted could get their money out through Switzerland.

The next world crisis will probably catch many by surprise too. Even if there were a minor crisis would you be ready for it? What happens if exchange controls are imposed tomorrow in the U.S.;

after all most countries already have them. If your assets are out of the crises area you can always delay compliance and even make it impossible for the government to ever seize those assets.

There is, of course, no guarantee that the next time trouble strikes Switzerland will be able to survive as it has in the past. Yet, there appears to be no alternative better suited to the task.

The Swiss respect money and they have developed a deep sense of responsibility to handle your funds conservatively and with discretion. The average Swiss banker is quite narrow minded and very conscious of his position as an intermediary and trustee. They are slow to change and rather stubborn in the pursuit of their goals. There are advantages and disadvantages to this.

The advantages are that the Swiss banker is extremely serious about his work. He will respect Swiss laws regarding secrecy to the letter and would never venture to compromise your trust in him. You will never find a Swiss banker moralizing about world affairs. He will pursue your business interests to their utmost as long as he too can profit from it.

The disadvantage is that the Swiss banker is often too worried about his image. Tradition prescribes that he stay out of the limelight and be careful not to alienate the public. An analogy can be drawn here to the political situation. The aim is to placate the group that is the biggest threat to survival. Hence we have a bank like Credit Swiss signing a secret agreement with the SEC regarding its clients in the U.S. It is a dangerous tendency if not moderated; we hope it does not continue.

There is no reason to be scared off from Swiss banks though. They can still offer the discretion and expert investment advice that they are famous for. You just have to be demanding. If one bank does not meet your needs try another. There is a considerable difference among banks in Switzerland that service foreign clients. Each has its own techniques and expertise and each attracts its own clientele.

In the section on accounts we will consider what options for investment are open to the account holder. From Switzerland you can trade on any major exchange in the world. For precious metals you may have the most active market in the world right here in Switzerland. For savings investments you have security and you have inflation fighters like a managed account, a Swiss bank fund and, of course, the Swiss franc.

In the following section we analyze the first steps to take in opening an account but do not forget to first review what purpose you hope to achieve by having a Swiss account and keep it in mind as you consider the next few chapters.

B. Opening an Account

The first step in opening an account is choosing a bank. Nearly all Swiss banks offer a wide range of services but most banks tend to specialize in a particular field. The exceptions to this are the five "Big Banks" which are able to handle just about any type of banking business that might be brought their way.

If you are considering having your firm open an account in Switzerland to actively do business in or through Switzerland then I would limit my choices to the three largest Swiss banks. There are, no doubt, other banks that may also be able to handle such accounts, but in terms of know-how and experience the Union Bank of Switzerland, Swiss Bank Corporation and Credit Swiss are the most qualified.

If you are an individual who is considering opening an account for personal or family reasons then the process of choosing a bank becomes more difficult. There are several obvious factors to consider:

1. Does the bank handle the type of account I want to have? In other words are they prepared to do the business I want to do through them?
2. How good is the bank? Is my money safe there? Reputation, size and age all enter in here.
3. How easy will it be for me to communicate with my bank? Are they, for example, used to having English speaking clients?

There are many other details you will also want to consider. Each person has different preferences. There is no set formula for finding the bank that suits you. One bank may be more "established" than another while one may have more foreign clients than another or one more liquidity than another; these are all determining factors, but never judge a bank solely on one or two criteria. In the past three years in Switzerland we have seen perhaps the most "established" (in terms of age and size) bank suffer over a one billion franc loss and we have seen a bank with a very high liquidity rating go under.

There are certain banks I would stay away from. Always, for example, be wary of the "it's too good to be true bank". The bank with the highest interest, the lowest commissions and the most flexibility is not always the best bank. That sounds very elementary but people are still being lured by what looks good rather than what is good. If possible it is also helpful to find out who or what is the controlling interest behind the bank. You will often find it is another Swiss bank or a multinational firm. Next step is to check them out.

I would be wary of small banks; in particular those that do not have another bank or firm standing behind them. They often lack experience and in times of trouble I am afraid they will be the first to go as fewer people will have an interest in keeping them solvent.

As an aside here I think it appropriate to discuss briefly the bankruptcy law in Switzerland. There is no federal insurance for bank deposits in Switzerland as there is in the U.S.A. (FDIC). Cantonal banks, however, do effectively have a cantonal guarantee which makes them certainly as safe, if not safer than any FDIC insured bank.

If however you have a savings or deposit account then according to Swiss Federal Bankruptcy Law, Article 219, your rights to these assets would be allocated to classes three to five (the last three classes) in the liquidation process after bankruptcy. Savings accounts are recognized under classes three and four up to a maximum value of 5000 Swiss francs in each class. Deposit accounts fall into the fifth class and could only be repaid after the creditors in the proceeding four classes had received full satisfaction.

These bankruptcy laws should be added encouragement to carefully choose your bank. There are crooks all over the world and in case one of them happens to be running the bank where you have deposited your money you could be in for trouble. About a dozen banks in Switzerland have gone out of business and declared bankruptcy in the past 15 years. In at least one case I know of the depositors were not fully repaid; in other cases there were naturally delays and interest payments had to be forfeited.

All this leads quite naturally to perhaps one of the most important steps to take when choosing a bank: the personal visit. There are many advantages to actually going to Switzerland and talking to your banker. The importance of this cannot be stressed enough, particularly if you are unfamiliar with Swiss banking services. By establishing personal contact you will be better able to judge the bank and its management. Likewise the personal visit makes it easier for the banker to be receptive to your needs as an investor. While in Switzerland you will also find it easier to gather background information on the bank you are considering. Do not hesitate to ask bankers what they think of their competitors.

I suggest writing to several banks that you may think would be most capable of serving you. These may be banks that you have heard or read about or you may choose among the banks I mention on the next page. Write them explaining what services you are looking for and ask them for literature on the different types of accounts they offer as well as if they have minimum deposit requirements for accounts. Be sure to also ask them for their most current balance sheet. It will help to judge their liquidity and size. (Remember their balance sheet will only show part of the picture; especially among banks that specialize in investment services their size will be very much understated. The most effective way of measuring bank size I know of is to compare the number of employees). Private banks issue no balance sheet.

After examining the literature plan a trip to Switzerland to visit several of the banks. Write or call ahead for an appointment with a manager or adviser (Kundenberater). You will find they are as anxious to meet you as you are them. Once there simply discuss your situation and listen to his advise. If you are not sure whether or not you should have a Swiss account this is the best time to find out. Have your questions ready you will be surprised at the different answers you will get, going from bank to bank. Do not be hesitant or feel intimidated if you are only planning on making a small deposit. The banks are there to serve you and if they do not give you that impression then they are not worthy of your hard earned money.

I have not made a sufficiently lengthy study of the various

banks in Switzerland to be able to present you with a complete list of alternatives. I think with a bit of common sense you are the best judge of which bank suits you. Rather than a complete list then I give you a list of banks which should be among those you consider.

For Commercial Transactions:

Swiss Bank Corporation
Aeschenvorstadt 1
4000 Basel

Union Bank of Switzerland
Bahnhofstrasse 45
8000 Zürich

Swiss Credit Bank
Paradeplatz 8
8000 Zürich

These three banks rank among the fifty largest in the world. They are experienced in all aspects of commercial and investment banking and have correspondent relations with banks literally all around the world.

I also include here Bank Leu, which is a small bank among the large banks, but is growing fast and has nearly the same capabilities as the other big banks but on a smaller scale.

Bank Leu
Bahnhofstrasse 32
8000 Zürich

For doing business in Switzerland:

Zürcher Kantonalbank
Bahnhofstrasse 9
8001 Zürich

Swiss Volksbank
Bahnhofstrasse 33
8001 Zürich

Kantonalbank von Bern
Bundesplatz 8
3000 Bern

These are all very substantial banks which are chiefly involved in servicing the domestic economy.

Investment — Service Banks.

These are the type of banks that are best able to serve an investor who wants security, discretion and conservative investment advice.

Julius Baer & Cie.
Bahnhofstrasse 36
8000 Zürich

Bordier & Cie.
Rue Hollande 16
Geneva

Foco Bank
Bellariastrasse 82
8038 Zürich

Bank Hofmann
Talstrasse 27
8001 Zürich

Lombard Odier & Cie.
Rue Corraterie 11
1200 Geneva

J. Vontobel
Bahnhofstrasse 3
8000 Zürich

Once you decide with which bank or banks you want to do business a number of practical problems will arise. You may ask yourself how do I transfer my funds to Switzerland? Are there reporting requirements; and if I want to keep my account secret how do I do it?

C. Getting Funds To Switzerland

Rather than discussing the insidious and often crooked means by which you might get your funds into Switzerland, we will discuss the legal way you can get your funds in.

I will just say in passing that some people seem to have a fixation with intrigue particularly when Swiss banks are involved and it often gets them into more trouble in the end than it was worth. There are intricate financial transactions that can be arranged and courier services from all over the world but if you are honest to begin with it is not worth the risk.

When considering the alternatives for getting money from abroad into Switzerland I will assume that we are transferring from a country with no direct control over capital transfer like the U.S. Should you be transferring from a country with exchange controls I suggest you pursue the matter with your banker when you visit Switzerland.

By Check:

You may send or bring in person a check to your bank. Cashiers checks and money orders are almost always accepted, although most banks will wait until the funds clear before crediting your account. Personal checks are, at times, also acceptable but the value date is usually set further ahead than on a cashiers check. Generally banks are somewhat hesitant to receive personal checks. Once you already have an account at the bank they will probably accept a personal check giving you immediate credit but again value dating the check ahead. You will be paying interest on the amount credited until the check clears.

If you mail a check remember to make it payable to yourself and endorse it. In either case, whether you bring it in person or send it, always keep a separate record of the check serial number so in case something should go wrong you can always place a stop payment on the check.

Cash:

Cash is the most obvious but also obviously the most dangerous way to transfer funds to Switzerland. There are two possibilities here: either deliver it yourself or have a courier deliver it. Couriers are usually associated with the illegal method of making payments abroad but as long as you declare the transaction and find a reliable courier there is nothing wrong with this method. Should you use a courier I suggest you have the courier put up a bond with you to cover the amount being sent. Should you decide to declare the funds and deliver the cash yourself you should keep the money carefully concealed; the less people that know the better, and be sure to arrive in Zürich when the banks are open.

Wire Transfer:

This is the simplest and probably quickest method. You simply ask the bank that is holding your funds abroad to transfer the money to your Swiss bank. You provide the bank with your name and the name of the Swiss bank and they will, through correspondant banks, send a coded telex message to your Swiss bank informing them that they have received a credit for X amount from you.

Do not forget to also send a message to your Swiss bank informing them what to do with the money once they receive it.

By the way, getting money back from Switzerland can be done using any one of these methods also.

Reporting Requirements:

There are basically two reporting requirements you have to concern yourself with if you have a Swiss account and you are a U.S. citizen. The first is the "Report of International Transportation of Currency and Monetary Instruments" and the second is a "Report of Foreign Bank and Financial Accounts". There is a third report, the "Currency Transaction Report" that will concern you but is not filed by you personally; more about this later.

These reporting requirements are a major hurdle to many who have a Swiss account. Part of the reason for having an account in Switzerland is in order to free some of your capital from controls and government interference. These reporting requirements are obviously counter to this reasoning. You should be well acquainted with these forms and be cognizant of the penalties for non-compliance.

In brief the requirements are as follows in:

U.S. Public Law 91-508

"...each person who physically transports, mails, or ships, or causes to be physically transported, mailed, shipped or received, currency or other monetary instruments in an aggregate amount exceeding $5,000 on any one occasion from the United States, or into the United States, must file U.S. Form 4790 with a U.S. Customs officer at any point of entry or mail the form to the Commissioner of Customs, Attn: Currency Transportation Reports, Washington, D.C. 20226."

The report must be filed the same day you mail the funds or if you leave the country and are carrying the funds on you, you are required to hand the completed form to the customs officer upon departure. If you receive the money in the mail you have 30 days to file the report.

Note that a transfer of funds by wire does not need to be reported. This is because the government will already have a record of this from the bank. This is also the case for cashier or personal checks. They are not required to be reported but you should be aware that the government will have a record through IRS form 4789, the Currency Transaction Report which will be filed by your bank for every transaction in excess of $10,000. Copies of both forms appear on the following pages.

Form **4790**
(Rev. May 1973)
Department of the Treasury
Internal Revenue Service

Report of International Transportation of Currency or Monetary Instruments
(PLEASE TYPE OR PRINT)

This form is to be filed with the Bureau of Customs

Part I   For Individual Departing From or Entering the United States

1 Name (last or family, first, and middle)

2 Identifying number (see instrs.)

3 Date of birth (month, day, and year)

4 Permanent address in United States or abroad

5 Of what country are you a citizen or subject?

6 Address while in the United States

7 Passport number and country

8 U.S. visa date

9 Place United States visa was issued

10 Immigration alien number, if any

COMPLETE EITHER 11(a) or 11(b) WHICHEVER IS APPLICABLE

11(a) I am departing from the United States at: (City) ....,
and my destination is: (City) .... (Country) ....

(b) I arrived in the United States at: (City) ....,
from this: (Foreign City)..., (Country) ....

Part II   For Person Shipping, Mailing or Receiving Currency or Monetary Instruments

12 Name (last or family, first, and middle) or business name

13 Identifying number (see instrs.)

14 Date of birth (month, day, and year)

15 Permanent address in United States or abroad

16 Of what country are you a citizen or subject?

17 Address while in the United States

18 Passport number and country

19 U.S. visa date

20 Place United States visa was issued

21 Immigration alien number, if any

22 The date of shipment or receipt of currency or instrument ▶ .... 19.....

23 The currency or monetary instrument was shipped ☐ to or received ☐ from ▶ ....
(Name)
....
(Address)

24 If the currency or monetary instrument was mailed, shipped, or transported, please complete the following:
(a) Method of shipment (Auto, U.S. Mail, Public Carrier, etc.) ▶ ....
(b) Name of transporter or carrier ▶

Part III   Currency and Monetary Instrument Information (See Instructions) (To be completed by everyone)

Type and amount of currency and/or monetary instrument:

Value in U.S. Dollars

25 (a) ☐ Coins . $
(b) ☐ Currency .
(c) ☐ Bearer instrument (specify type) ▶ ....
(d) Total amount (add lines (a), (b) and (c)) . $

26 If other than United States currency is involved, please complete the following: (See instructions)
(a) Currency name ▶   (b) Country ▶

Part IV   General—To be Completed by All Travelers, Shippers and Recipients

27 Were you acting as an agent, attorney, or in other capacity for anyone in this currency or monetary instrument activity? .   ☐ Yes   ☐ No

If "Yes," please complete the following:
(a) Name of person in whose behalf you are acting ▶ ....
(b) Complete address of that person ▶ ....

(c) Business activity, occupation or profession of that person ▶
Under penalties of perjury, I declare that I have examined this report, and to the best of my knowledge and belief it is true, correct and complete.

Sign here ▶ --
Signature

(Title, if applicable)

Date

General Instructions

This report is required by Treasury Department regulations (31 Code of Federal Regulations 103).

Who Must File.—Each person who physically transports, mails, or ships, or causes to be physically transported, mailed, shipped or received currency or other monetary instruments in an aggregate amount exceeding $5,000 on any one occasion from the United States to any place outside the United States, or into the United States from any place outside the United States.

A TRANSFER OF FUNDS THROUGH NORMAL BANKING PROCEDURES WHICH DOES NOT INVOLVE THE PHYSICAL TRANSPORTATION OF CURRENCY OR MONETARY INSTRUMENTS IS NOT REQUIRED TO BE REPORTED.

Exceptions.—The following persons are not required to file reports: (1) a Federal reserve bank, (2) a bank, a foreign bank, or a broker or dealer in securities in respect to currency or other monetary instruments mailed or shipped through the postal service or by common carrier, (3) a commercial bank or trust company organized under the laws of any State or of the United States with respect to overland shipments of currency or monetary instruments shipped to or received from an established customer maintaining a deposit relationship with the bank, in amounts which the bank may reasonably conclude do not exceed amounts commensurate with the customary conduct of the business, industry or profession of the customer concerned, (4) a person who is not a citizen or resident of the United States in respect to currency or other monetary instruments mailed or shipped from abroad to a bank or broker or dealer in securities through the postal service or by common carrier, (5) a common carrier of passengers in respect to currency or other monetary instruments in the possession of its passengers, (6) a common carrier of goods in respect to shipments of currency or monetary instruments not declared to be such by the shipper, (7) a travelers' check issuer or its agent in respect to the transportation of travelers' checks prior to their delivery to selling agents for eventual sale to the public, nor by (8) a person engaged as a business in the transportation of currency, monetary instruments and other commercial papers with respect to the transportation of currency or other monetary instruments overland between established offices of banks or brokers or dealers in securities and foreign persons.

When and Where to File:

A. *Recipients.*—Each person who receives currency or other monetary instruments shall file Form 4790, within 30 days after receipt, with the Customs officer in charge at any port of entry or departure or by mail with the Commissioner of Customs, Attention: Currency Transportation Reports, Washington, D.C. 20226.

B. *Shippers or Mailers.*—If the currency or other monetary instrument does not accompany the person entering or departing the United States, Form 4790 may be filed by mail on or before the date of entry, departure, mailing, or shipping with the Commissioner of Customs, Attention: Currency Transportation Reports, Washington, D.C. 20226.

C. *Travelers.*—Travelers carrying currency or other monetary instruments with them shall file Form 4790 at the time of entry into the United States or the time of departure from the United States with the Customs officer in charge at any Customs port of entry or departure.

An additional report of a particular transportation, mailing, or shipping of currency or other monetary instruments, is not required if a complete and truthful report has already been filed. However, no person otherwise required to file a report shall be excused from liability for failure to do so if, in fact, a complete and truthful report has not been filed. Forms may be obtained from any Internal Revenue or Bureau of Customs office.

PENALTIES.—Civil and criminal penalties, including under certain circumstances a fine of not more than $500,000 and imprisonment of not more than five years, are provided for failure to file a report, supply information, and for filing a false or fraudulent report. In addition, the currency or monetary instrument may be subject to seizure and forfeiture. See sections 103.47, 103.48 and 103.49 of the regulations.

Definitions

Bank.—Each agent, agency, branch or office within the United States of a foreign bank and each agency, branch or office within the United States of any person doing business in one or more of the capacities listed:

(1) a commercial bank or trust company organized under the laws of any state or of the United States;

(2) a private bank;

(3) a savings and loan association or a building and loan association organized under the laws of any state or of the United States;

(4) an insured institution as defined in section 401 of the National Housing Act;

(5) a savings bank, industrial bank or other thrift institution;

(6) a credit union organized under the laws of any state or of the United States; and

(7) any other organization chartered under the banking laws of any state and subject to the supervision of the bank supervisory authorities of a state.

☆ GPO—1973—458-217/37-0746135

Foreign Bank.—A bank organized under foreign law, or an agency, branch or office located outside the United States of a bank. The term does not include an agent, agency, branch or office within the United States of a bank organized under foreign law.

Broker or Dealer in Securities.—A broker or dealer in securities, registered or required to be registered with the Securities and Exchange Commission under the Securities Exchange Act of 1934.

IDENTIFYING NUMBER.—Individuals should enter their social security number, if any. However, aliens who do not have a social security number should enter passport or alien registration number. All others should enter their employer identification number.

Investment Security.—An instrument which: (1) is issued in bearer or registered form; (2) is of a type commonly dealt in upon securities exchanges or markets or commonly recognized in any area in which it is issued or dealt in as a medium for investment; (3) is either one of a class or series or by its terms is divisible into a class or series of instruments; and (4) evidences a share, participation or other interest in property or in an enterprise or evidences an obligation of the issuer.

Monetary Instruments.—Coin or currency of the United States or of any other country, travelers' checks, money orders, investment securities in bearer form or otherwise in such form that title thereto passes upon delivery, and negotiable instruments (except warehouse receipts or bills of lading) in bearer form or otherwise in such form that title passes upon delivery. The term does not include bank checks made payable to the order of a named person which have not been endorsed or which bear restrictive endorsements.

Person.—An individual, a corporation, a partnership, a trust or estate, a joint stock company, an association, a syndicate, joint venture, or other unincorporated organization or group, and all entities cognizable as legal personalities.

Special Instructions

You should complete each line which applies to you.

Part II.—Line 22, Enter the exact date you shipped or received currency or the monetary instrument(s).

Line 23, Check the applicable box and give the complete name and address of the shipper or recipient.

Part III.—Line 26, If currency or monetary instruments of more than one country is involved, attach a schedule showing each kind, country, and amount.

Form **4789**
(April 1972)
(Replaces TCR-1)
Department of the Treasury
Internal Revenue Service

Currency Transaction Report

File a separate report for each transaction
(Complete all applicable parts—see instructions)

Part I   Identity of person who conducted this transaction with the financial institution

Name (Last, first and middle initial)

Social security number

Number and street

Business, occupation or profession

City or town, State and ZIP code

Part II   Person or organization for whom this transaction was completed (Complete only if different than Part I)

Name

Identifying number

Number and street

Business, occupation or profession

City or town, State and ZIP code

Part III   Description of transaction (If additional space is needed, attach a separate schedule)

1. Nature of transaction (check the applicable boxes)
   - ☐ Deposit
   - ☐ Withdrawal
   - ☐ Currency exchange
   - ☐ Check cashed
   - ☐ Check purchased
   - ☐ Traveler's checks purchased
   - ☐ Security purchase (specify) ....
   - ☐ Other (specify)

2. Total amount of currency transaction (in U.S. dollars)

3. Amount in denominations of $100 or higher

4. Date of transaction (Month, day and year)

5. If other than U.S. currency is involved, please furnish the following information:

Currency name

Country

Total amount of foreign currency

6. If a check was involved in this transaction, please furnish the following information (See instructions):

Date and amount of check

Payee

Drawer of check

Drawee bank and City of location

Part IV   Type of identification presented in this transaction

By customers:
- ☐ Savings account number..................
- ☐ Checking account number..................
- ☐ Share account number..................
- ☐ Loan account number..................
- ☐ Safety deposit box number..................
- ☐ Other (specify)

By others:
- ☐ Driver's permit   State   Number
- ☐ Passport   Country   Number
- ☐ Alien ID card   Country   Number
- ☐ Other (specify)

Part V   Financial institution reporting the financial transaction

Name and address

Identifying number (see instructions)

Business activity

Sign here ▶   Authorized signature   Title   Date

General Instructions

This report is required by Treasury Department regulations (31 Code of Federal Regulations 103).

Who Must File.—Beginning July 1, 1972, each financial institution (as described in these instructions) shall file a report of each deposit, withdrawal, exchange of currency or other payment or transfer, by, through, or to such financial institution, which involves a transaction in currency of more than $10,000.

Exceptions.—Financial institutions are not required to file Form 4789 for transactions:

(1) with Federal Reserve Banks or Federal Home Loan Banks;

(2) solely with, or originated by, financial institutions or foreign banks; or

(3) between a bank and established customers maintaining a deposit relationship with the bank, in amounts which the bank may reasonably conclude do not exceed amounts commensurate with the customary conduct of the customer's business, industry or profession.

However, upon request each bank shall submit a report listing those customers who engage in transactions which were not reported because of the exemption in (3).

When and Where to File.—This report shall be filed on or before the 45th day following the date of the transaction with the Internal Revenue Service Center, 11601 Roosevelt Boulevard, Philadelphia, Pennsylvania 19155. Forms may be obtained from any Internal Revenue Service office.

Identifying Number.—Social security number or employer identification number if other than individual.

Identification Required.—Before any transaction is effected a financial institution shall verify and record the identity, and record the account number on its books or the social security or taxpayer identification number, if any, of a person with whom or for whose account such transaction is to be effected. Verification of identity for a customer of the financial institution depositing or withdrawing funds may be by reference to his account or other number on the books of the institution. Verification of identity in any other case may be by examination, for example, of a driver's license, passport, alien identification card, or other appropriate document normally acceptable as a means of identification.

Penalties.—Civil and criminal penalties are provided for failure to file a report or to supply information, and for filing a false or fraudulent report. See sections 103.47 and 103.49 of the regulations.

Specific Instructions

Part I.—(1) In the address block, enter the permanent address of the person conducting the transaction.

(2) In the social security block, enter the social security number of the person conducting the transaction. If the person has no number, write "None" in this block.

Part II.—(1) In the name block, individuals should enter their last name, first name and middle initial, if any, in that order. All others should enter their complete organization name.

(2) In the identifying number block, enter the social security number or employer identification number.

Part III, line 6.—This part should be completed only where a check is cashed or a bank check is purchased with currency.

Part IV.—See instruction "Identification Required," above.

Part V.—Institutions may also enter in the name and address block other identifying information.

Definitions

Bank.—Each agent, agency, branch or office within the United States of a foreign bank and each agency, branch or office within the United States of any person doing business in one or more of the capacities listed below:

(1) a commercial bank or trust company organized under the laws of any state or of the United States;

(2) a private bank;

(3) a savings and loan association or a building and loan association organized under the laws of any state or of the United States;

(4) an insured institution as defined in section 401 of the National Housing Act;

(5) a savings bank, industrial bank or other thrift institution;

(6) a credit union organized under the laws of any state or of the United States; and

(7) any other organization chartered under the banking laws of any state and subject to the supervision of the bank supervisory authorities of a state.

Currency.—The coin and currency of the United States or of any other country, which circulate in and are customarily used and accepted as money in the country in which issued. It includes United States silver certificates, United States notes and Federal Reserve notes, but does not include bank checks or other negotiable instruments not customarily accepted as money.

Financial Institution.—Each agency, branch or office within the United States of any person doing business in one or more of the capacities listed below:

(1) a bank;

(2) a broker or dealer in securities, registered or required to be registered with the Securities and Exchange Commission under the Securities Exchange Act of 1934;

(3) a person who engages as a business in dealing in or exchanging currency as, for example, a dealer in foreign exchange or a person engaged primarily in the cashing of checks;

(4) a person who engages as a business in the issuing, selling or redeeming of travelers' checks, money orders, or similar instruments, except one who does so as a selling agent exclusively, or as an incidental part of another business;

(5) an operator of a credit card system which issues, or authorizes the issuance of, credit cards that may be used for the acquisition of monetary instruments, goods, or services outside the United States.

(6) a licensed transmitter of funds, or other person engaged in the business of transmitting funds abroad for others.

Person.—An individual, a corporation, a partnership, a trust or estate, a joint stock company, an association, a syndicate, joint venture, or other unincorporated organization or group, and all entities cognizable as legal personalities.

Transaction in Currency.—A transaction involving the physical transfer of currency from one person to another. A transaction which is a transfer of funds by means of bank check, bank draft, wire transfer, or other written order, and which does not include the physical transfer of currency is not a transaction in currency within the meaning of this part.

I have included copies of both forms to make it clear how comprehensive the requirements are. I have heard lawyers and investment advisers come up with "suggestions" for legally avoiding the requirement. Many of them I believe never read the requirements. Be extremely careful if you follow such advice; remember the government has many sources to choose from should they decide to investigate you. Following a lawyer's "suggestion" may only draw the government's attention to you. The less attention you draw to yourself the better. After all, do you really think they follow up each of the hundreds of thousands of reports they receive each week?

Narrow interpretations of the law are possible, of course, but stay within the limits of common sense or the only one you may be outsmarting in the long run is yourself.

Furthermore, before you go through a lot of trouble to hide the transmittal of funds to Switzerland you should keep in mind that all foreign bank accounts must be reported on your income tax return and Form 90-22.1 must be filed. I urge you to carefully read the definition of "Bank Financial Accounts" on the form. You will see it too is quite comprehensive. The definition includes all deposit accounts, certificates of deposit, loans and security accounts; also notice that the term "other financial accounts" includes commodity accounts. Some banks argue that gold claim accounts do not fit under this rubric; what do you think? Even if an account is not in your name but you have "signature authority," that is to say "control its disposition" (Section H, Paragraph 1), you are required to report it.

What all this boils down to is that if you want privacy from government knowledge regarding your financial transactions you will find it almost impossible to accomplish legally. Possibly you might want to consider sending a number of cashiers checks individually each under $5,000 and then holding the funds abroad in a safe deposit box. There would be no reporting requirement and you would be perfectly legal. Another, more sensible, course is that when you are in doubt as to legality in a transaction present it to your lawyer for an opinion. If he says it is legal get a letter from him stating that and keep it in your files; should conditions change you could always plead innocence by presenting his legal opinion. First, however, make sure you can trust your lawyer.

Before leaving this section it seems appropriate here to make a general comment about reporting requirements and having a Swiss bank account. Whatever course you decide to take in regard to your privacy be sure that once you have committed yourself to a decision you stick by it. As one banker I know recently told a group of investors, "In regards to your Swiss bank account be either black or white but not gray." If after weighing your prognosis for the future along with the legal repercussions of your actions you decide, for example, not to complete the reporting requirements then do not ever put yourself in a position where you later want to justify your actions.

This reasoning is especially relevant to those who want a Swiss account for the secrecy it offers: once committed never compromise your position. Do not keep any records of your account or related activities, do not even accept mail that might link you to your account and most importantly never tell anyone who does not have to know. Your Swiss banker does not.

D. Initial Paper Work

Although it used to be relatively simple matter to open your account by mail this is no longer the case. There are now several banks that will not send signature cards abroad. You may have to appear personally at the bank to open your account. Swiss banks are now required to be much more careful about who they accept money from. As was already mentioned in the section on banking secrecy the following conditions must be met before a bank can accept an account (from the agreement between the Swiss National Bank and the Swiss Banking Association, December 9, 1977):

1. The bank must be certain of the identity of the account holder.
2. The bank is not to accept any funds that would make improper use of banking secrecy, that is, funds that were illegally obtained in the view of Swiss law.
3. A bank is not to actively aid in capital transfers from countries where such transfers are illegal, nor is a bank to issue misleading or falsified documents to aid a customer in evading taxes.

Form Approved
OMB No. 48-RO-546

Department of the Treasury
Form 90-22.1 (9-78)
SUPERSEDES ALL PREVIOUS EDITIONS

REPORT OF FOREIGN BANK AND FINANCIAL ACCOUNTS

For the calendar year 19 . . . .

OFFICIAL USE ONLY

This form should be used to report financial interest in or signature authority or other authority over one or more bank accounts, securities accounts, or other financial accounts in foreign countries as required by Department of the Treasury Regulations (31 CFR 103). You are not required to file a report if the aggregate value of the accounts did not exceed $1,000. Check all appropriate boxes. SEE INSTRUCTIONS ON BACK FOR DEFINITIONS.

1. Name (Last, First, Middle)	2. Social security number or employer identification number if other than individual	3. Name in item 1 refers to
4. Address (Street, City, State, Country, ZIP)		☐ Individual ☐ Partnership ☐ Corporation ☐ Fiduciary

5. ☐ I had signature authority or other authority over one or more foreign accounts, but I had no "financial interest" in such accounts (see instruction J). Indicate for these accounts.

(a)   Name and social security number or taxpayer identification number of each owner

(b)   Address of each owner

(Do not complete item 9 for these accounts)

6. ☐ I had a "financial interest" in one or more foreign accounts owned by a domestic corporation, partnership or trust which is required to file Form 90-22.1. (See instruction L). Indicate for these accounts.

(a)   Name and taxpayer identification number of each such corporation, partnership or trust

(b)   Address of each such corporation, partnership or trust

(Do not complete item 9 for these accounts)

7. ☐ I had a "financial interest" in one or more foreign accounts, but the total maximum value of these accounts (see instruction I) did not exceed $10,000 at any time during the year. (If you checked this box, do not complete item 9.)

8. ☐ I had a "financial interest" in 25 or more foreign accounts. (If you checked this box, do not complete item 9.)

9. If you had a "financial interest" in one or more but fewer than 25 foreign accounts which are required to be reported, and the total maximum value of the accounts exceeded $10,000 during the year (see instruction I), write the total number of those accounts here
Complete items (a) through (f) below for one of the accounts and attach a separate Form 90-22.1 for each of the others.
Items 1, 2, 3, 9, and 10 must be completed for each account. Check here if this is an attachment. ☐

(a) Name in which account is maintained	(b) Name of bank or other person with whom account is maintained
(c) Number and other account designation, if any	(d) Address of office or branch where account is maintained

(e) Type of account. (If not certain of English name for the type of account, give the foreign language name and describe the nature of the account. Attach additional sheets if necessary.)

☐ Bank Account   ☐ Securities Account   ☐ Other (specify) . . . .

(f) Maximum value of account (see instruction I)

☐ Under $10,000   ☐ $10,000 to $50,000   ☐ $50,000 to $100,000   ☐ Over $100,000

10. Signature	11. Title (Not necessary if reporting personal account)	12. Date

PRIVACY ACT NOTIFICATION

Pursuant to the requirements of Public Law 93-579, (Privacy Act of 1974), notice is hereby given that the authority to collect information on Form 90-22.1 in accordance with 5 U.S.C. 552(e)(3) is Public Law 91-508, 31 U.S.C. 1121, 5 U.S.C. 301, 31 CFR Part 103.

The principal purpose for collecting the information is to assure maintenance of reports or records where such reports or records have a high degree of usefulness in criminal, tax, or regulatory investigations or proceedings. The information collected may be provided to those officers and employees of any constituent unit of the Department of the Treasury who have a need for the records in the performance of their duties. The records may be referred to any other department or agency of the Federal Government upon the request of the head of such department or agency for use in a criminal, tax, or regulatory investigation or proceeding.

Disclosure of this information is mandatory. Civil and criminal penalties, including under certain circumstances a fine of not more than $500,000 and imprisonment of not more than five years, are provided for failure to file a report, supply information, and for filing a false or fraudulent report.

Disclosure of the social security number is mandatory. The authority to collect this number is 31 CFR 103. The social security number will be used as a means to identify the individual who files the report.

INSTRUCTIONS

A. Who Must File a Report—Each United States person who has a financial interest in or signature authority or other authority over bank, securities, or other financial accounts in a foreign country, which exceeded $1,000 in aggregate value at any time during the calendar year, must report that relationship each calendar year by filing Form 90-22.1 with the Department of the Treasury on or before June 30, of the succeeding year.

An officer or employee of a commercial bank which is subject to the supervision of the Comptroller of the Currency, the Board of Governors of the Federal Reserve System, or the Federal Deposit Insurance Corporation need not report that he has signature or other authority over a foreign bank, securities or other financial account maintained by the bank unless he has a personal financial interest in the account.

In addition, an officer or employee of a domestic corporation whose securities are listed upon national securities exchanges or which has assets exceeding $1 million and 500 or more shareholders of record need not file such a report concerning his signature authority over a foreign financial account of the corporation, if he has no personal financial interest in the account and has been advised in writing by the chief financial officer of the corporation that the corporation has filed a current report which includes that account.

B. United States Person—The term "United States person" means (1) a citizen or resident of the United States, (2) a domestic partnership, (3) a domestic corporation, or (4) a domestic estate or trust.

C. When and where to File—This report shall be filed on or before June 30 each calendar year with the Department of the Treasury, Post Office Box 28309, Central Station, Washington, D.C. 20005.

D. Account in a Foreign Country—A "foreign country" includes all geographical areas located outside the United States, Guam, Puerto Rico, and the Virgin Islands.

Report any account maintained with a bank (except a military banking facility as defined in instruction E) or broker or dealer in securities that is located in a foreign country, even if it is a part of a United States bank or other institution. Do not report any account maintained with a branch, agency, or other office of a foreign bank of other institution that is located in the United States, Guam, Puerto Rico, and the Virgin Islands.

E. Military Banking Facility—Do not consider as an account in a foreign country, an account in an institution known as a "United States military banking facility" (or "United States military finance facility") operated by a United States financial institution designated by the United States Government to serve U.S. Government installations abroad, even if the United States military banking facility is located in a foreign country.

F. Bank, Financial Account—The term "bank account" means a savings, demand, checking, deposit, loan or any other account maintained with a financial institution or other person engaged in the business of banking. It includes certificates of deposit.

The term "securities account" means an account maintained with a financial institution or other person who buys,

sells, holds, or trades stock or other securities for the benefit of another.

The term "other financial account" means any other account maintained with a financial institution or other person who accepts deposits, exchanges or transmits funds, or acts as a broker or dealer for future transactions in any commodity on (or subject to the rules of) a commodity exchange or association.

G. Financial Interest—A financial interest in a bank, securities, or other financial account in a foreign country means an interest described in either of the following two paragraphs:

(1) A United States person has a financial interest in each account for which such person is the owner of records or has legal title, whether the account is maintained for his or her own benefit or for the benefit of others including non-United States persons. If an account is maintained in the name of two persons jointly, or if several persons each own a partial interest in an account, each of those United States persons has a financial interest in that account.

(2) A United States person has a financial interest in each bank, securities, or other financial account in a foreign country for which the owner of record or holder of legal title is: (a) a person acting as an agent, nominee, attorney, or in some other capacity on behalf of the U.S. person, (b) a corporation in which the United States person owns directly or indirectly more than 50 percent of the total value of shares of stock; (c) a partnership in which the United States person owns an interest in more than 50 percent of the profits (distributive share of income); or (d) a trust in which the United States person either has a present beneficial interest in more than 50 percent of the assets or from which such person receives more than 50 percent of the current income.

H. Signature or Other Authority Over an Account—

Signature Authority—A person has signature authority over an account if such person can control the disposition of money or other property in it by delivery of a document containing his or her signature (or his or her signature and that of one or more other persons) to the bank or other person with whom the account is maintained.

Other authority exists in a person who can exercise comparable power over an account by direct communication to the bank or other person with whom the account is maintained, either orally or by some other means.

I. Account Valuation—For items 7, 9, and Instruction A, the maximum value of an account is the largest amount of currency and non-monetary assets that appear on any quarterly or more frequent account statement issued for the applicable year. If periodic account statements are not so issued, the maximum account asset value is the largest amount of currency and non-monetary assets in the account at any time during the year. Convert foreign currency by using the official exchange rate at the end of the year. In valuing currency of a country that uses multiple exchange rates, use the rate which would apply if the currency in the account were converted into United States dollars at the close of the calendar year.

The value of stock, other securities or other non-monetary assets in an account reported on Form 90-22.1 is the fair market value at the end of the calendar year, or if withdrawn from the account, at the time of the withdrawal.

For purposes of items 7, 9, and Instruction A, if you had a financial interest in more than one account, each account is to be valued separately in accordance with the foregoing two paragraphs.

If you had a financial interest in one or more but fewer than 25 accounts, and you are unable to determine whether the maximum value of these accounts exceeded $10,000 at any time during the year, check item 9 (do not check item 7) and complete Item 9 for each of these accounts.

J. United States Persons with Authority Over but No Interest in an Account—Except as provided in Instruction A and the following paragraph, you must state the name, address, and identifying number of each owner of an account over which you had authority, but if you check item 5 for more than one account of the same owner, you need identify the owner only once.

If you check item 5 for one or more accounts in which no United States person had a financial interest, you may state on the first line of this item, in lieu of supplying information about the owner, "No U.S. person had any financial interest in the foreign accounts." This statement must be based upon the actual belief of the person filing this form after he or she has taken reasonable measures to endure its correctness.

If you check item 5 for accounts owned by a domestic corporation and its domestic and/or foreign subsidiaries, you may treat them as one owner and write in the space provided, the name of the parent corporation, followed by "and related entities," and the identifying number and address of the parent corporation.

K. Consolidated Reporting—A corporation which owns directly or indirectly more than 50 percent interest in one or more other entities will be permitted to file a consolidated report on Form 90-22.1, on behalf of itself and such other entities provided that a listing of them is made part of the consolidated report. Such reports should be signed by an authorized official of the parent corporation.

If the group of entities covered by a consolidated report has a financial interest in 25 or more foreign financial accounts, the reporting corporation need only note that fact on the form; it will, however, be required to provide detailed information concerning each account when so requested by the Secretary or his delegate.

L. Avoiding Duplicate Reporting—If you had financial interest (as defined in instruction G(2)(b), (c) or (d) in one or more accounts which are owned by a domestic corporation, partnership or trust which is required to file Form 90-22.1 with respect to these accounts in lieu of completing item 9 for each account you may check item 6 and provide the required information.

M. Providing Additional Information—Any person who does not complete item 9, shall when requested by the Department of the Treasury provide the information called for in item 9.

N. Signature (Item 10)—*This report must be signed* by the person named in Item 1. If the report is being filed on behalf of a partnership, corporation, or fiduciary, it must be signed by an authorized individual.

O. Penalties—For criminal penalties for failure to file a report, supply information, and for filing a false or fraudulent report see 31 U.S.C. 1058, 31 U.S.C. 1059, and 18 U.S.C. 1001.

The banks are very serious about enforcing these regulations and a regulatory commission has been set up in Zürich under the supervision of the Swiss National Bank. Banks that openly violate the provisions of this agreement are liable to receive a fine of up to 10 million Swiss francs.

If you keep in mind the pervasive importance of banking in Switzerland and the practical necessity of maintaining neutrality, you will realize this agreement, in fact, should do little to change the status quo. It is largely aimed at placating the opponents of Swiss banking secrecy and it also gives the banks an added degree of legitamacy.

The new agreement simply makes the requirements more stringent and acts as a warning to those who want to use Swiss banking as a whitewash for their criminality.

Despite comments to the contrary this agreement results in no effective change in Swiss banking secrecy. At most it makes it more difficult for some people to open an account and it also means there may be a few more forms for you to sign. Realize that once you have the account all the information you have given and the existence of your account remains protected under Swiss law.

To open an account you may have to sign any one of a number of forms. I say may because the requirements vary from bank to bank depending on how strictly the bank interprets the agreement. You will certainly have to sign a signature card and some sort of agreement in which you acknowledge the General Banking Conditions: a declaration that you understand banking secrecy cannot claim absolute validity, a power of attorney or limited power of attorney, a declaration for correspondence to be held at the bank, and a letter of indemnity. I also suggest you ask your bank for an explanation of Swiss National Bank restrictions that may affect your account (see chapter on Capital Controls). Now a quick review of the various forms you may encounter:

General Banking Conditions

This will vary somewhat from bank to bank. You can expect to find here information regarding the following:
    Conditions regarding signatures, legitimation and power of
        disposition.
    Extent of bank responsibility.
    Recourse against bank errors or omissions.
    Applicable law and jurisdiction
    Regulations for the safe custody of securities and other
        valuables.

Declaration regarding banking secrecy:

Whether or not you will have to sign such an understanding depends on how strictly the bank you are dealing with interprets its agreement with the National Bank and on how closely the National Bank is watching your bank. There is no doubt that certain of the larger, more established banks have a better working relationship with the Swiss National Bank and the Federal Banking Commission than do new and smaller banks. The larger banks are often under less pressure to directly comply with regulation as it is felt they can better regulate themselves internally, with supervision, of course. As a result some of these banks do not require their customers to sign such an agreement.

The agreement poses no threat to your security even if you sign it. It simply highlights the exceptions to banking secrecy (see chapter on bank secrecy) and requires that the account holder has made "no improper use of banking secrecy . . . . in particular to [hide] criminal acquisition of the assets."

We had earlier discussed that a good way to maintain secrecy was to have a lawyer act as trustee to open your account; in this way you were protected not only by the banking law but also by the professional secrecy of the lawyer. This agreement is also supposed to pierce this veil, to the extent that the lawyer must testify to the trustworthiness and legality of the account holder. Banks will no longer accept such testimony from just any lawyer as they once did. The bank must feel your lawyer is trustworthy and honest in his appraisals if they are to accept your account.

ACCOUNT APPLICATION FORM
BANK NB
SWITZERLAND
☐ Mr.   ☐ Mrs.   ☐ Ms.

First name: _____ _____Last name: ⌐_____

Date of birth: _____Nationality:_____

Passport no :_____Profession:_____

Address: _____

Country: _____ Telephone:_____

Type of account:

	Currency				
	SFr	US $	Can $	DM	Other
☐ Current account (checking account)	☐	☐	☐	☐	_____
☐ Deposit account	☐	☐	☐	☐	_____
☐ Commodity account (precious metals)	☐	☐	☐	☐	_____
☐ Safekeeping account (securities and other valuables)	☐	☐	☐	☐	_____
☐ Other _____	☐	☐	☐	☐	_____

Carry the   ☐ in my/our name(s)   ☐ under a number
account:
              ☐ an individual account   ☐ a joint account
              the account holder may
              give power of attorney
              to other persons by
              having them sign on
              the signature card
Correspondence: ☐ to be mailed to _____
                ☐ to be held at bank

Language: _____ _ —

Special Instructions: _____

Unless otherwise agreed, all transactions in the currency mentioned—between the clients or their attorneys shall be carried out by means of this account notwithstanding its designation. All accounts, including deposit accounts, shall be governed by the same rules and regulations concerning correspondence and right of signature.

I/we the undersigned acknowledge that all transactions shall be governed by the general conditions of the bank. Moreover, I/we confirm having taken notice of the conditions, the regulations for the safe custody of securities and other valuables and the regulations governing the signature card printed on the reverse side.

I/We furthermore confirm that the given details are true and correct.

Place and date: _____
Signature(s) of
account holder(s): _____
Signed in the
presence of: _____
(signature)
Recommended by: _____ _____
(If no signature cards are received the above signature(s) of the account holder(s) shall be valid)

BANK NB SWITZERLAND

General Conditions

The following conditions are intended to clearly regulate the relations between the bank and its customers.

1. Power of Disposition

The signatures and signing powers given in writing to the bank are alone valid insofar as the bank is concerned until cancelled in writing, notwithstanding entries to the contrary in the Register of Commerce or other media of public notice.

2. Objections of the Customer

Any objection by the customer relating to the execution or non-execution of any order of any kind as well as any objection to any statement of account or of deposit, or to any other communication, must be made promptly upon receipt of the respective communication, but at the latest within the time specified by the bank; in case of non-receipt of any communication the customer must make his complaint at the time when he should have received the communication through the usual postal channels.

3. Communications of the Bank

Communications of the bank are deemed to have been made if dispatched to the last address notified by the customer. The date indicated on the copy or on the mailing records in the possession of the bank is presumed to be the date of dispatch. Mail which is to be kept in deposit at the bank is—in case of doubt—considered to have been delivered at the date it bears.

4. Verification of the Signatures and the Legitimation

Any damage resulting from reliance by the Bank upon any false, forged, altered or otherwise legally insufficient instructions, documentation or other legitimation shall be borne by the customer, unless the Bank is guilty of gross negligence.

5. Legal Incapacity

Any damage resulting from legal incapacity of the customer or of a third party must be borne by the customer, unless such incapacity has been published in an official journal in Switzerland in the case of the customer himself or has been communicated to the bank in writing in the case of a third party.

6. Errors in Transmission

Any damage resulting from the use of the mails, telegraph, telephone, telex, of any other system of communication or means of transportation, especially from losses, delays, misunderstandings, mutilations or duplicates, must be borne by the customer, unless the bank is guilty of gross negligence.

7. Non-execution or Belated Execution of Orders

In case of damage due to non-execution or belated execution of orders (stock exchange orders excluded), the bank is liable for the loss of interest only, unless it has been warned in the particular case of the imminent risk of more extensive damages.

8. Right of Pledge and Right of Compensation

With respect to all assets which it holds in custody for account of the customer, either at its own offices or elsewhere, the bank has a lien for all its unliquidated claims originating in the banking relationship, irrespective of maturity or currency and a right to immediate compensation for all liquidated claims. This rule applies equally to credits and to loans with or without guarantees or securities. In as far as papers are not made out to the bearer, they are hereby pledged to the bank. Upon default of performance on the part of the customer, the bank may, in its discretion, realize upon the pledges by formal proceedings or by private arrangements.

9. Current Account Relations

The bank credits and debits interests, commissions and fees agreed upon or customary, as well as taxes, at its choice, quarterly, semi-annually or annually. The bank reserves the right to modify its rates of commissions and interest at any time, in particular if the conditions on the money-market have changed, and to inform the customer of any modification in an appropriate way. Should several orders have been given by the client, the total amount of which would exceed his credit balance available or the credit granted to him, the bank is entitled to decide in its discretion which of these

orders, regardless of their dates or the time they were received, are to be carried out in full or in part.

In the absence of presented objection within one month, the statements of account issued by the bank are deemed to have been approved, even if the form of acknowledgment to be signed by the customer has not been received by the bank.

The express or tacit approval of the statement of account includes the approval of all items, as well as of any possible reservation of the bank contained therein.

The counterpart corresponding to the **credit balances in foreign currencies** are deposited in the name of the bank, but for account and at the risk of the customer—proportionately up to his share—with correspondents considered good by the bank within or outside the currency area in question. The customer bears in particular the risk of legal or administrative restrictions and charges.

The customer may dispose of his credit balances in foreign currencies by selling them, by drawing and cashing checks and by transfers, in any other way however only with the consent of the bank. For cash payments or withdrawals in the currency of the account the bank may charge a commission.

10. Bills of Exchange, Checks and other Instruments

The bank reserves the right to redebit bills of exchange which have been discounted or credited under the reserve of final payment. For unpaid bills of exchange, checks and other papers the bank is at liberty to assert its right of recourse either by debiting the current account or without regard to any existing account. Nevertheless, until the final settlement of any existing debit balance, the bank retains against the world the right to claims arising out of the Law of Bills of Exchange or the Check Law or otherwise for payment of the full amount of the bills of exchange and checks and of all other instruments, as well as accessory claims against everybody liable on the paper.

11. Termination of the Business Relationship

The bank reserves the right to cancel any business relationships, in particular credits which have been promised or granted, with immediate effect, in which case any possible claims of the bank will immediately become due for repayment, unless other agreements have been made.

12. Saturdays equivalent to Legal Holidays

For all business relations with the bank, Saturdays are equivalent to legal holidays.

13. Applicable Law and Jurisdiction

All legal aspects of the relationship between client and bank shall be governed by **Swiss law**. The place of performance, the place for prosecution of clients domiciled abroad, as well as the **exclusive jurisdiction of lawsuits and any other kinds of legal proceedings, shall be Zurich, excepting only that the Bank may sue the client in any competent court at the domicile of the client or in any other court having jurisdiction.**

14. Reservation of Special Regulations

Apart from the present general conditions special regulations stipulated by the bank apply to certain transactions, especially to the safe custody and administration of securities and of valuables (safe custody regulations); to the hiring of safes; to the use of check books; to savings, deposit and placement books, deposit and salary accounts; and to mortgage loans.

Moreover, stock exchange transactions are subject to the local rules, documentary transactions to the Uniform Customs and Practice for Commercial Documentary Credits issued by the International Chamber of Commerce, and collecting and discounting transcations to the general terms issued by the Association of Swiss Bankers.

15. Modifications of the General Conditions

The bank reserves the right to modify the general conditions at any time. The customer will be informed of these modifications by circular letter or in any other appropriate way, and in the absence of opposition within a month, the modifications are deemed to have been approved.

Declaration on Opening an Account or a Deposit of Securities

The undersigned hereby declares:

☐ that he is acting for own account

☐ that he is acting for account of the following person(3):

Name(s)	Christian name(s)	Domicile	Country

☐ that he is acting as mandatary legally bound by professional secrecy, or as trustee. In that capacity he confirms that he knows personally the beneficial owner of the assets to be deposited with the bank and that, in ascertaining the origin of such assets with all reasonable care and diligence, he has not become aware of any circumstance that would point to any improper use of banking secrecy by the person entitled, in particular to criminal acquisition of the assets in question.

☐ that the domicile-establishing company represented by him is controlled by the following natural persons:

Name(s)	Christian name(s)	Domicile	Country

Mark with a cross what is applicable

The undersigned takes cognizance of the fact that banking secrecy, legally protected under Art. 47 of the Federal Law on Banks and Savings Banks, cannot claim absolute validity: the organs, employees and mandataries of the bank are liable to give evidence and information vis-à-vis the authorities, inasmuch as federal and cantonal regulations provide for an obligation to give evidence or information (for instance in criminal proceedings). This also applies vis-à-vis authorities of foreign countries to the extent to which the Swiss Confederation has pledged itself vis-à-vis other states to grant legal aid.

The undersigned finally takes note that the establishment of accounts and securities deposits maintained under numbers or passwords is a purely internal measure by the bank affecting in no way its obligation vis-à-vis authorities to give evidence or information.

Place, Date _____ Signature _____

Name and Exact Address _____
(Please Print)
_____

12.78 5000   Translation (Original Text: German)

Depending on the amount of discretion you are striving for, I would not worry too much about signing such an agreement personally, but would certainly try to avoid it. After all, it is one more document linking you to the account.

Power of Attorney

This brings us into the realm of control over your account. There are several options. You can if you wish open a joint account in which case be sure to have the two or more signatures that are applicable to the account appear on the signature card. Such accounts can be drawn up so that one or more signatures are necessary in order to effect a transaction with the account. Note a power of attorney is for unlimited duration and will continue even after your death if not revoked.

A Power of Attorney gives the recipient all right over the account "to dispose of assets, purchase, sell, pledge, withdraw securities ... to sign contracts ... This power includes also dispositions made by said Attorney in his/her favor." In other words, it is the same as having a joint account with the signature of the "attorney" having equal power over the account. (p. 149)

Limited Power of Attorney

Limited power of attorney is often recognized by Swiss banks. In practice a limited power of attorney could place any of a number of restraints on the recipient. For example, he/she could control the purchase or sale of securities, precious metals, and currencies in the account but would not have the right to withdraw any such assets from the account without your signature. This is usually the preferred form of granting a power of attorney to an investment adviser or to the bank itself should you choose to have a managed account with them.

Declaration for Holding Mail

This simply states that you instruct the bank to hold all correspondence at the bank on your behalf. The mail is kept at

BANK NB SWITZERLAND

Power of Attorney

(please print)

I/We the undersigned _____

residing at _____

_____

here by grant BANK NB Zürich (hereinafter called "the Bank") full powers with a view to represent me/us validly within the limitations of the following provisions:

The bank is authorized to dispose, on behalf of the principal(s), of the securities and assets whatsoever of the undersigned principal(s), lodged with the bank, insofar as these deposits and assets may be increased or reduced as a result of purchases, sales or conversions of securities, and for this purpose any possible subscription rights may be exercised or sold at best.

The bank is furthermore authorized, in a general manner, to do everything it will deem necessary or appropriate for the management of the assets lodged with the bank.

But the bank is not authorized to carry out, in any way whatsoever, any withdrawals of all or part of the funds and securities deposited or to pledge the assets and securities in question; nor is it empowered to order bonuses, except when these are destined for taking over securities of an equivalent amount.

The principal(s) expressly approve(s), and they/he do(es) so in advance, all acts of management or abstentions of the bank and recognize(s) that the bank does not assume any responsibility whatsoever for the consequences of the transactions which the bank, acting in good faith, will have made or will have abstained from making. In addition, the principal(s) undertake(s) to compensate the bank for any expenses or damages it might have incurred on account of this power of attorney.

This power of attorney will remain valid until and unless revoked in writing.

It is expressly agreed that this power of attorney will not become void upon the death or loss of exercise of the civil rights of the principal(s), but will continue in full effect (Swiss Federal Code of Obligations, Article 35).

The parties agree that the constitution and validity of this power of attorney are governed by Swiss law and that transactions carried out by virtue of the said power of attorney will be judged in accordance with such law. Any litigations between the parties will be brought before the competent courts of the Canton of Zürich. The Bank, however, is authorized to assert its claims at the legal domicile of the principal(s).

Place   Date

_____

Signature(s) of the principal(s): _____

_____

Account Nr.: _____

the bank in a folder and is considered delivered as of the date carried on the communication. The bank destroys any correspondence which is not collected within five years.

This measure is again to insure your privacy. If you want to keep your account secret you should make use of this option. Remember be black or white but not gray.

Letter of Indemnity

In a letter of indemnity the account holder stipulates that he will, instead of using his normal signature, sign under a pseudonym or other symbol. The holder of the account must assume the full risk of signing in this matter and indemnify the bank and/or third parties for any damages that might arise from this.

Restrictions Affecting Account (for foreigners)

In the chapter on capital controls we discussed a number of restrictions that had been in effect in 1978. As of the time this work is being completed many of these restrictions have been lifted. We anticipate that the restrictions of the size of Swiss franc deposits as well as commission charges on balances in an account of over Sfr. 100,000.00 will continue. The scope of these restrictions is not discussed here as it is covered in a later chapter. It is important to keep up to date with changes in these restrictions as they could have a significant impact on your holdings. Once you have an account the bank should keep you apprised of the situation.

E. If an Account Holder Dies?

There are two easy ways to transfer your account to an heir. One is the signature card; the other through the power of attorney. If you have an account and your heir has signature rights over the account whether from the signature card or from a

Part of the old town on River Limmat at Zürich with the churches of St. Peter's and Fraunmünster

power of attorney, then at your death the heir still has control over the account and if he/she wishes can have the account reopened in his/her name. This, of course, is the easiest way to effect a transfer but many account holders do not want their heir either to know about the account or to have free access to it while the account holder is still alive. Under Swiss law there is no such thing as a trust account as known in the U.S. and Canada.

There are other options. Something I have seen many clients do is to get the signature of their heir unwittingly on a power of attorney. You can clip the signature of the heir from another paper and tape it onto the power of attorney. Your next step would be to write a letter to your heir, to be opened at the time of your death, that would inform him/her of the fact that he/she has power of attorney over an account in Switzerland. Give the letter to your lawyer and instruct him to present the letter to your heir at your death. Be sure to make it clear with which bank the money is, the account number and instructions for claiming the money.

If you have not reported your account and are keeping it a secret I would suggest keeping the letter with a lawyer in Switzerland. Laws can always change, and, in any case, there is no reason for any lawyer to know the contents of the letter. Depending on how educated your heir is in financial matters I would also describe the legal status of the account with instructions of what to do with the funds. This is a very delicate matter, because what is right in one case is not necessarily right in another. After your death the account is your heirs' problem but it would be a shame to have them lose it out of stupidity.

At the time of your death, unless you had previously made arrangements to the contrary, your account will be part of your estate. There are no inheritance taxes imposed on non-residents by the Swiss Government. There are, however, inheritance taxes in the U.S., Canada, and the U.K. all of which will effect you if you are from any one of these countries.

What happens if you made no provision to transfer your account? There are the famous stories about accounts that were opened during the Second World War and have never been claimed since. Of course, this can happen if you are keeping your account a secret. The bank will continue to hold your assets until such time as an heir or relative makes a claim to them. If not, the bank will not make any attempt to contact any of your heirs or relatives. If you have made no provisions to transfer your account but heirs or relatives know of the account, they can make a claim to it by providing the bank with the following:

1. A court order naming the legal heir(s).
2. A notarized death certificate.
3. Instructions from the executor with a notarized copy of the last will (if applicable).
4. Positive identification on the part of the heirs.

These are the essentials, again some banks may require more, some less.

By special arrangement some banks are prepared to assume the administration and distribution of estates, the execution and safekeeping of last wills and inheritance agreements. You will have to check with your banker for more details about this.

F. Types of Accounts

The types of accounts available at Swiss banks vary somewhat in their conditions, their benefits and their titles, but basically most of the banks can offer any one of the type of accounts we discuss here below.

The Current Account

A current account is your basical holding account. In many ways it is similar to what is called a checking account in the U.S. and Canada. The basic features are that the balance standing to a customer's credit on current account is repayable on demand and that there is a right to draw checks against this account. As I have already mentioned, checks are not very popular in Switzerland, and abroad it will be difficult to cash checks drawn on a bank in Switzerland because of the time it will take the check to clear.

Current accounts can be held in any one of a number of different convertible currencies apart from Swiss francs. Always be careful to inform your bank which currency account you want to credit if you are depositing funds and have accounts in more than one currency. These accounts are usually balanced quarterly

Bahnhofstrasse—Zürich

and you will find commission charges are quite small if any.

Interest on current accounts is available at some, but not all, banks. The interest rates are not as favourable as those that can be earned on Swiss francs in a savings type account nor as favourable as the interest earned on fiduciary type accounts in foreign currencies.

Unless you are going to have a large turnover in your account a current account is not for you. Firms need it in order to conduct day to day business but an individual investor should only make use of this as a holdover account.

Variations on current accounts

As I mentioned above it is possible to earn interest on a current account that is in all but name a current account. (Sometimes it is called a private account). There may be a minimum deposit requirement to earn interest on such an account. Alternatively there will be limits on withdrawal during a specific time period. However, if funds are being withdrawn to purchase securities or precious metals through the bank then there are usually no withdrawal limitations. The interest paid on such accounts is subject to the 35% Swiss withholding tax, which will be automatically deducted by the bank. There will probably be commission charges for such accounts but they should not exceed 20.00 Swiss francs per year. If a private investor needs to make use only periodically of a current account I urge him to investigate the possibility of such a modified current account.

Savings Accounts

Savings accounts are the most practical way for the foreign investor to hold Swiss francs. The present interest rate offered on normal savings accounts is 2% per annum, less the 35% Swiss federal withholding tax on the interest earned. Up to SF 5,000.00 may be withdrawn per month. You are required to give six months notice if you plan on withdrawing a larger amount. Again, just as in the case of a modified current account, you can withdraw any amount if you use it to purchase securities or precious metals through the bank. Also, as in the case of the modified current account, or any interest earning account for that matter, the maximum amount of Swiss francs you can earn interest on is SF 100,000.00. For amounts held over SF 100,000.00 you are charged a negative interest rate of 2.5% per quarter.

Some foreigners have complained that the interest rate offered on Swiss francs is too low. After compensation for inflation, however, that has not at all been the case as the interest rate represents an actual real savings rate of nearly 2%. In Argentina you could have opened an account in the local currency and earned 95% interest, but in real terms that could have represented as low as a 40% interest on savings rate. In the U.S. savings accounts earn about 6% per annum but the inflation rate is nearly 14%. The situation in Switzerland will also change somewhat in the coming years as we can expect inflation to develop slightly in Switzerland also. As long as savings accounts can offer a positive real rate of return, though, they are anything but a bad investment.

The interest paid on savings accounts is the same at all banks as it is fixed by general agreement (the Zinskonvenium). Savings accounts are available at most all banks in Switzerland. There is such a thing as pure savings banks and they are distinct from the big banks and investment banks in that they are severely limited by law as to how they can invest their depositors funds. Furthermore, savings banks have the advantage of being able to issue bearer savings books (Sparhefte). However, as a foreigner you would find it difficult to get such an account.

Other specifics on savings accounts:

1. Savings accounts in Switzerland have a privileged status in the case of bankruptcy up to a total amount of SF 10,000.00.
2. Savings accounts are generally not available in foreign currencies.
3. No commission charges but there may be a charge every time a statement has to be issued.
4. Foreigners are limited to one savings account per household.

Investment Savings Account (Anlagesparkonto)

This is very similar to a standard savings account except that the withdrawal restrictions are more severe and the interest rate paid higher. At present the interest rate on the investment savings account is 1/4% higher than the interest offered on normal savings accounts. This interest is also subject to the withholding tax. The withdrawal restrictions are up to SF 10,000.00 per calendar year. Six months notice is needed if you plan a larger withdrawal without penalty. The purchase of securities or precious metals through the bank is not directly possible through this account. However, the larger banks will allow you to purchase bonds and shares of their own bank up to any amount for this account without having to give previous notice.

Senior Citizens Savings Accounts

The withdrawal conditions covering this account are the same as those covering a normal savings account. Up to SF 5,000.00 may be withdrawn per month; six months notice for larger amounts. Purchase of securities and precious metals through banks are permitted without notice.The interest rate offered is at present also 1/4% above that offered on straight savings accounts (again less withholding tax). The only condition here is that the account holder must be 60 years or older to gain the benefit of this account.

Both the senior citizens account and the investment savings account are presently only available in Swiss francs.

Fixed or Time Deposit

A fixed or time deposit is one in which you agree to leave your funds with the bank for a fixed period anywhere from three months to several years. In return for this commitment the bank will offer a higher rate of interest than on savings accounts. Unfortunately for foreign investors time deposits in Swiss francs are not now available to non-residents. I suspect that this National Bank regulation will be with us for quite some time, at least as long as the Swiss franc retains its appeal.

Fiduciary Deposits

Fiduciary deposits have become increasingly popular with foreign investors and increasingly more attractive as the Euro-currency market has developed.

The fiduciary deposit is a deposit in which the interest rate is fixed for as long as the funds remain in the Euromarket. Fiduciary deposits have maturity of two days, one month, two months, six months, nine months or one year. Under normal circumstances you are not allowed to withdraw the funds before the maturity date.

There is a minimum deposit requirement for such accounts. The minimum requirement varies somewhat from bank to bank and is also dependent on the foreign exchange markets. Generally we can say that you need at least U.S. $50,000.00 or equivalent before you can even consider such an account.

The funds that you present your Swiss bank with are not really on deposit with them at all. Your Swiss bank will place your funds in the Euromarket under their name. The funds are placed through your bank with a well-established bank abroad; for example, Deutsche Bank in Germany or Credit Lyonnais in France. Your Swiss bank is in effect lending your money to the foreign bank for you.

These deposits are available in all major convertible currencies like the U.S.$, the French Franc, Deutsche Mark, Dutch Guilder, British Pound, and others. The interest rate paid on these deposits is better than on normal bank deposits. There is no federal withdrawing tax as the interest is earned outside of Switzerland.

The larger interest rate that you earn may be offset by the fact that a fiduciary deposit can be quite risky in times of crisis. The funds that you invest in a fiduciary deposit are not a liability of your Swiss bank and should the bank you have lent your money to default, then you stand a good chance of losing your investment. If there is ever a large financial crisis and a collapse of the Euromarket, banks would protect their depositors first if they could, and fiduciary deposits would have a very low priority.

In order that the client understands these risks, and the mechanism behind the fiduciary deposit, banks ask the account holder to sign a fiduciary agreement before placing the funds.

Fiduciary Agreement

AGREEMENT

between

Name: (please print)

_____
(hereinafter referred to as the "Client")

and the

BANK NB Switzerland
(hereinafter referred to as the "Bank")

1. The Client hereby instructs the Bank to effect capital investments in the form of time deposits with foreign banks judged to be reliable by the Bank, in its own name, but for the account and at the risk of the Client. The Bank acts as Agent within the meaning of Article 394 ff of the Swiss Federal Code of Obligations.

2. The amount, the debtor and the terms of the investments involved shall be designated from case to case.

In the absence of specific or standing instructions, which should reach the Bank at the latest one week before the due date, the Bank shall automatically renew at maturity existing investments (principal as well as interest) under deduction of the usual fiduciaty commission. The Bank is authorized to choose the deposit bank, the duration, the currency and the interest conditions at discretion in the best of the clients interest, but without any obligation on the Bank's part.

3. The Client places the capital at the disposal of the Bank before the latter assumes any commitment in respect to a foreign bank. The Bank has the sole obligation of assigning to the Client such claims as it receives in the form of repayment of principal and of interest. The Bank is under no obligation to perform any other services.

4. If the foreign bank does not fulfill its commitments or fulfills them only partially, the Bank then has the sole obligation of assigning to the Client the claims held on his behalf.

5. This agreement will not cease by reason of loss of capacity to act nor by death but it will retain its validity until written revocation to the Bank.

6. All legal aspects of the relationship between the Client and the Bank shall be governed by Swiss law. The place of performance, as well as the exclusive place of jurisdiction of lawsuits and other kinds of legal proceedings shall be Zurich or Geneva, (excepting only that the Bank may sue the Client in any competent court at the domocile of the Client or any other court having jurisdiction).

_____   _____
(Place)   (Date)

                                         Signature: (Client)

                                         _____

                                         _____

                                         Account Number

                                         _____

You will notice in the fiduciary agreement that, in the absence of any instructions, the bank will automatically renew the fiduciary deposit. If you do not sign the fiduciary agreement you are subject to the 35% withholding tax.

Bank charges for arranging a fiduciary deposit for you are between 1/4% to 1/2% per annum. Since the deposit is placed with the foreign bank in the name of your bank you never have to worry about your anonymity being compromised. If you are considering such an account I suggest keeping it with a fairly short maturity. In times of instability you should not be locked into any long term fixed interest investments.

There is one more thing that should be said before we leave this section on fiduciary accounts. As already mentioned, it is not possible to place a fiduciary deposit in Swiss francs through Switzerland. However, many of the banks have branches or affiliates outside of Switzerland which could open a fiduciary deposit for you in Swiss francs outside of Switzerland and then lend the money to a bank in Switzerland in their name. You should realize though, that because of the high rate of bank liquidity in Switzerland, interest rates paid for Swiss francs are quite low, at present only a fraction of a percent per annum for short maturities. This would only interest someone who wants to hold a lot of Swiss francs for investment purposes. I would then suggest you investigate banking in a country like Austria. Banking secrecy is also in the criminal code there.[1]

You can hold Swiss franc deposits in Austria without any restrictions; there is no negative interest and no withholding tax on the interest of Swiss franc deposits. On the other hand Austria is not Switzerland and, if you want, there are ways to keep rather substantial amounts of Swiss francs in Switzerland. If you are interested in banking elsewhere in Europe, however, I suggest looking at the literature of some Austrian banks. For example:

Bankhaus Deak & Co. Ltd.
Rathausstrasse 20, Dept. A50
A-1010 Vienna

Certificates of Deposit

While we are in the realm of fixed interest deposits I thought we would cover both Certificates of Deposit and Kassenobligationen here.

Certificates of deposit are available in most currencies except for the Swiss franc in Switzerland. Interest rate paid is similar to that paid on fiduciary deposits and maturities are from three months on. There is no withholding tax on CD's as long as they are issued by banks abroad. You do have a stamp tax on the certificate which comes to .15% of the principal. Certificates of deposit usually require a minimum deposit of at least U. S. $ 5,000. The bank charges between 1/3 and 1/4% brokerage commission. The big difference between a fiduciary deposit and a CD is that the CD's are issued in your name and CD's also have, to a limited extent, a secondary market.

Kassenobligationen

On a per capita basis the Swiss are the most heavily mortgaged people in the world. The Kassenobligationen are the main way for the banks to finance their mortgages. The maturity of the bonds is from three to seven years. The interest rate on the bonds with seven years maturity is about 1 to 1 1/2 % above the current savings account rate and is indicative of the expected inflation rate. There is a 35% withholding tax on the interest earned. They are sold in units of 1000 and 5000 Swiss francs. It is recommended that the bonds are kept in a safekeeping account. Normally only 1/2 the normal safekeeping fee is charged if you keep the Kassenobligationen with the bank where you bought them.

Managed or Discretionary Accounts

These are accounts in which you place your funds with your bank for them to invest on your behalf and at their discretion. In order to maintain such an account you need a minimum balance which may vary from   US$ 25,000. to   US$ 100,000. or even more at some private banks. You are required to complete a Power of Attorney giving the bank the right to make transactions

TABLE NO. 9

Comparative Interest Rate *

Fiduciary deposit in Euromarket:

	1 Month	2 Months	3 Months	6 Months	1 Year
$	14	15	15⅛	15⅛	14
£	17	17	16¾	16¼	15⅜
DM	8⅛	8⅞	8¾	8¾	8⅜
hfl.	9¾	10¼	10¼	10¼	9⅞

Certificates of Deposit:

	3 Months	6 Months	1 Year
US$	13¼	13⅜	13½
£	14½	14⅝	14¾
DM	7¾	8	8¼
hfl.	9⅛	9¾	9½

* Indication only, as of November 1979

for you. In effect, the bank will act as your investment manager.

Swiss bankers enjoy a good reputation when it comes to such managed accounts. This is due to the conservative nature of their investments, the fact that they maintain an international outlook on investments and, perhaps most importantly, they have been able generally to maintain good rates of return for their clients. Realize, however, that few people know exactly how well these managed accounts perform and although I know of cases where there have been several years of 25% return on capital, I also know of cases where there have been losses of 50% per year. Usually, though, these accounts perform moderately well. Swiss bankers are more likely to be safe than sorry. The private banks make their living from these managed accounts and usually they are dealing with sizable family fortunes. Their goal is to preserve the wealth of their clients rather than to seek high rates of return.

You should visit several porfolio managers before making any decision. Again a trip to Switzerland will be necessary. Because of SEC regulations Swiss banks can not openly discuss such accounts in the U.S. and they will not take the risk. Once in Switzerland set up an appointment and ask the portfolio manager what he would plan to do with your funds. Find someone whose investment strategy parallels your own. If you do not see eye to eye with your investment advisor you will not be able to maintain your trust in him. No banker is infallible but the idea behind portfolio management is that you should be able to sleep at night.

Bank charges for discretionary accounts varies from 0 to 1%. Usually you will find the charges to be about 1/4% or less; remember the bank is already earning commissions on every transaction.

Bond and Stock Investment Trusts

To much of the English speaking world our investment trusts are known as mutual funds. We have already mentioned them in an earlier chapter. They provide a small investor with the advantages of diversification that a large investor has. On the other hand this should not be confused with portfolio management. After all a portfolio may be diversified between bonds, stocks, precious metals and real estate, while an investment trust will be either in bonds or stocks. The investment trusts will distinguish between bonds and stocks within Switzerland and those outside of Switzerland. On the average the performance in either category has been mediocre. There have been restrictions on the purchase of Swiss bonds and stocks by non-residents and although these restrictions are no longer in effect they did manage to dampen a lot of the interest in investment trusts. The big banks maintain the most diversified portfolios although their returns are not necessarily that good. You should realize that at present some of these funds are still not available to U.S. investors. (See opposite page)

Safekeeping Accounts

This account is used for the safekeeping of securities and other valuables. Annual charges for the safekeeping and administration of securities (clipping coupons, redemption, etc.) are approximately .15% of the market value of the securities. Such safekeeping accounts are protected by the same banking secrecy law that covers other accounts. (See p. 166)

Something interesting that people have done is to put a sum of money in an envelope and have the bank hold it for them in a safekeeping account. Certain banks will withdraw funds from the envelope if you request it and leave the remainder in the account. It is always possible to seal an envelope and present it to your bank for safekeeping.   There is a 4 franc charge plus .15% per year on the declared market value of the contents.

Another possibility available at the bigger banks is keeping your own safe deposit box. It is also possible to get insurance coverage for the contents. The premium is about 1/2% on the declared value. is also possible to leave the key to your safe deposit box at the bank. The charge is about 10 francs and your key is placed in an envelope and treated as a safekeeping deposit. When you want your key you go to the bank, sign for the key where they hold safekeeping accounts and then proceed to your safe deposit box. When you are through replace the key in the envelope and return it. Safe deposit boxes can also be held under a number rather than a name.

Performance of a representative fund:

American Valor* (Swiss Mutual Fund for American Securities):

Income distributed as a percent of net asset value
(Per unit in S.F.)

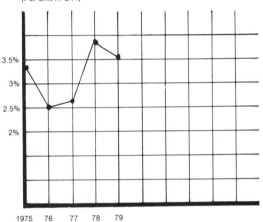

Swiss Valor* (Swiss Mutual Fund for Swiss Securities):

Income distributed as a percent of net asset value
(per unit in S.F.)

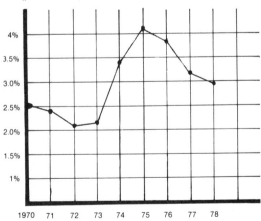

*Fund Management Société Internationale de Placements Basle
Fund Custodian Bank: Swiss Bank Corporation, Zürich

Safe Custody Regulations

governing the safekeeping and administration of securities and other items.

Bank NB Ltd., hereinafter referred to as "the Bank" will take into safe custody and administer securities of all kinds and items in an open safekeeping account subject to the following terms and conditions:

1. Safekeeping

The Bank undertakes to keep the securities and items entrusted to it in a safe place and to devote to them the same care as it does to its own.

The depositor agrees that the Bank is entitled to keep his securities and precious metals in a collective safe or to entrust them to a central depository. Securities which are registered in the name of the owner as well as securities and valuable items which have to be kept separately for other reasons will be excluded from collective safekeeping.

Unless otherwise agreed, the Bank shall arrange for the safekeeping and administration of securities deposited abroad in the Bank's name but at owner's risk and expense, by a foreign bank or an institution recognized by banks which engage in the safekeeping of securities.

Each depositor enjoys co-ownership of the holdings in Switzerland prorated as per the values he has deposited.

If the securities are deposited abroad they will be subject to the laws and practices of the respective place of safekeeping.

In case of drawings of securities held in a central depository the bank will divide the drawn securities among the depositors, using a method for this second drawing which will guarantee all beneficiaries an equal chance to be taken into account as at the original drawing.

2. Administration

Without specific instructions from the client, the Bank undertakes:

(a) to collect and to employ respectively matured interest and dividend coupons;

(b) to supervise drawings, redemptions, conversions and amortisations of securities as well as to collect securities being redeemed in accordance with available publications and lists without, however, assuming any responsibility in this respect;

(c) to obtain new coupon sheets and to exchange temporary certificates against definitive securities;

(d) to receive capital and interest payments for account of the depositor insofar as the debtors have been instructed to make such payments to the Bank.

In agreement with the depositor, the Bank will further handle:

(e) conversions;

(f) payments on securities not fully paid up;

(g) calls on and collection of mortgages and other securities;

(h) the exercise or sale of subscription rights to new securities. Unless the Bank has received the client's instructions to the contrary by the day preceding the last stock-exchange notice regarding the subscription right or, in the case of unlisted or foreign securities, within reasonable time, the Bank shall be entitled to sell such subscription rights at the best figure without assuming any responsibility therefor.

3. Statements

The Bank will send to the depositor annually, as a rule as at the end of a calendar year, a statement of his safekeeping account for verification. Unless objection is raised within four weeks from the date of mailing, such statements will be deemed to have been approved.

4. Power of operating and Authentication of Signatures

Instructions regarding the power to sign given to the Bank in writing will be deemed to be valid, irrespective of entries in the commercial register or publications to some other effect, until the Bank has received written notice of revocation. Unless the Bank is guilty of gross negligence, the client shall bear any loss due to the nonrecognition of absence of legitimation or to forgery.

5. Power of Attorney

A power of attorney of unlimited duration is fully effective until the Bank receives a written notice of revocation.

6. Lien

In the event that the client becomes a debtor of the Bank, the securities deposited will serve as a collateral for the Bank's claim to the extent that the Bank may deem it necessary to have security therefor.

7. Withdrawal

Withdrawal of securities will be made against the depositor's receipt. The Bank is entitled, but not obligated, to demand that identification papers be produced.

8. Transport Insurance

Unless the client otherwise disposes in time, the Bank will insure, at the client's expense, the transport of securities and other items to the extent that such is customary and possible within the framework of the Bank's own insurance.

9. Safekeeping Fees

The safekeeping fees will be calculated in accordance with the tariff in force.

The Bank reserves the right of changing the rates at any time. The Bank may separately charge for exceptional services and costs as well as for postage and other disbursements.

For securities deposited outside the Bank, the fees of outside depositaries, postage, cable, teleprinter and telephone fees will be charged to the depositor.

No charge is made for the safekeeping and administration of shares of Bank NB. The charge made for safekeeping and administering deposit certificates of Bank NB 's reduced to one half of the rate in effect.

10. Administration of Estates, Last Wills

By special agreement, the Bank is prepared to assume the administration of entire estates and to handle the distribution of estates, the execution of wills and the safekeeping of last wills, inheritance agreements and the like.

11. Bank Secrecy

The bank officers and employees are legally bound to keep the client's banking transactions in utmost secrecy.

12. Amendments to these Regulations

The Bank reserves the right at any time to amend these regulations. The depositor will be notified of such amendments by circular letter or in any other appropriate manner. Amendments will be deemed to have been approved unless objection is raised within one month.

13. Notification to Depositors

All notices of the Bank shall be deemed to have been served if mailed to the client's last known address. The date of the copies or mailing lists in the Bank's possession is considered as the date of mailing in cases of doubt. Mail to be withheld by the Bank is considered to have been mailed, in cases of doubt, at the date of the correspondence involved.

14. Applicable Law and Place of Venue

All rights and obligations arising from the safekeeping contract shall be governed **by Swiss law. Zurich 1** shall be the place of performance and debt collection from clients residing abroad, and the venue for all actions. The Bank is also entitled to take legal steps against the client with the court having jurisdiction at the client's place of residence or with any court having jurisdiction.

CHAPTER 14

The Gold Market and Gold Accounts

A lot of people who have accounts in Switzerland do so because they want to take advantage of Swiss banking experience in trading precious metals particularly gold and silver. For decades the Swiss bankers have been hard money advocates and proponents of the monetary function of gold. For investment advisors or bankers elsewhere gold is a speculative metal, but to the Swiss bankers and their customers gold is a store of value, a hedge against chaos and inflation. That is not to say you Swiss banker will want you to put all your assets into precious metals but he certainly will suggest you put some of your holdings into precious metals "just in case." For people who have their assets in currencies of countries that suffered from inflation such advice has paid off well in the last half century.

The Gold Market

The Swiss banks may very well be the major market for gold in the world. We can never know for sure because there is no information available on what volume of gold is traded daily in Zürich and Geneva. Again the big banks are the major market makers. The big three: Credit Swiss, Swiss Bank Corporation and Union Bank of Switzerland are in the so called gold pool and in effect, they act as agents to sell gold for the gold producing nations who sell through Zürich. Every week, for example, there are Swissair flights arriving at Kloten airport delivering gold from South Africa to be sold through the gold pool. We also have in Zürich the Wozchod Handelsbank A.G. which is the Russian bank that represents the Russian government in their gold sales. You should immediately notice a difference here between the Swiss market and that of, say, the New York Comex. Much of the

Comex volume is in the futures market, whereas in Switzerland we trade spot gold. That is not to say that at the end of each day vast quantities of gold are being shifted around; that is not necessary. But it does mean that much of the world's gold is held in Switzerland.

If you were able to take a tour of the gold operations at one of the big banks or at one of the other large banks actively trading gold day to day you would probably be quite surprised by the things you see. In the trading room you would view a large trading desk with up to a dozen traders battling a battery of telephones and keeping up to date on the latest developments of their news screens, teletypes and other information monitors. A manager at the head of the table directs the overall strategy keeping his traders up to date on what the bank's overall position is. Ideally the bank wants to do as little speculating as possible, rather they would like to match their buy and sells and come out at the end of the day with only a small position long or short on their own accounts. If the manager feels he can ride a trend and the bank's managers agree, the bank may, for a short time, take a position of its own. It is no secret that banks in Switzerland and abroad have learned some hard lessons from such speculation. Particularly for the Swiss have to be careful when they purchase gold, say in London against U.S. dollars, that they cover their foreign exchange position as well.

Prices that the traders trade with on the phones or over the telex machines are quoted in dollars per bar, dollars per ounce, Swiss franc per kilogram, or in some cases even some other combination. The conversion formulas are as follows:

number of grams multiplied by .03215=number of troy ounces
number of troy ounces multipled by 31.1042=number of grams
(1000 grams = 1 kilogram)

Both bid and sell prices are always given, the spread varies in relation with the anxiety felt in the market. Each offer to buy and sell is good for up to ten bars. A bar, which is the standard trading unit, is approximately 400 ounces or 12 1/2 kilos and of at least 999.9 fineness. At $500/ounce one bar is worth $200,000.00. Each trader can easily trade several hundred bars a day.

The morning begins by reading the latest news and discussing a strategy. Calls are placed to Hong Kong, which is just closing, to get a feel for the market there. The trading in Zürich begins at nine and continues until shortly before the London fixing at 10:00 a.m. Trading resumes after the fixing, pauses for the afternoon fixing and then continues right through the opening of the gold market in New York. The market for gold is a 24 hour market linked by telephones and teleprinter machines.

At the end of the day the settlements are made. Usually this is only a matter of making a bookkeeping entry. The banks that are the big gold dealers all have accounts with each other. The trades at the end of the day often cancel each other or are covered by deposits in their respective accounts. Not too many actual physical deliveries need to be made, although this too can be the case.

Bars that are delivered must, as we have already said, be of 999.9 fineness or better and be approximately 12.5 kilos in weight. If you were to visit the vault where such gold is held you would see bars from South Africa, the Soviet Union, the United States and the United Kingdom. The Russian bars are favored because they are always of the highest purity (other bars often have to be discounted for the junk metals they contain) and their exact weight (to four decimal places) is neatly stamped on each bar.

Obviously few investors would be able to purchase gold in multiples of standard bars. On the other hand, it is not economically feasible to split up the gold bars every time someone wants a smaller amount. There are kilo bars available and some other sizes that are also traded but this is more the exception than the rule.

In a basic gold account you purchase the gold and the bank subscribes a part of a gold bar to you equal to the value of the gold purchased. This is known as a custodial account and is for all practical purposes the same as a safekeeping account. The bank is only storing the gold for you. The gold bar or fraction thereof which has been appropriated for you is solely your property. This gold is not part of the bank's balance sheet; should something go wrong with the bank it cannnot use this gold to pay off its' debts.

Depending on the bank such gold may be physically segregated from other gold holdings of the bank. You must inquire at your bank if you wish to take advantage of this additional service.

The charges are somewhat higher than on a regular custodial account and for a segregated account it is necessary for you to purchase a bar or bars of size one kilogram, 100 or 400 ounces. The charges on a custodial account are as for a safekeeping account, about 1.50 Swiss francs for each 1,000.00 francs of market value; for larger amounts this fee is reduced. For segregated accounts the safekeeping fees go up an additional 50%. It is of course always possible to purchase a gold bar and have it put in a safe deposit box; if you own a substantial amount of gold bullion this is probably a course worth investigating. Remember, though, the safekeeping fee includes insurance, whereas if you kept the gold in your own safe deposit box you would have to make arrangements for insurance on your own.

There is another type of account called a claim account. It should be called the gimmick account. For all practical purposes this, too, is like a custodial or safekeeping account, with one difference—you do not actually take title to the gold. The bank buys the gold for you and you receive a claim to the gold. The gold is yours but you only have a claim to it while the bank has title. It is said that claim accounts exist because a bank may not want to take delivery on gold that it knows a client wants to shortly resell. So, instead the bank lays claim to the gold asking whomever the bank buys the gold from to set it aside. However, even with a claim account you can receive the gold at your bank if you would want delivery. In my opinion this is no different than a regular custodial account. Banks never take delivery of all the gold they own as they have holdings for their trading in accounts at other banks anyhow. The gimmick with the claim account is that you might be able to say you own no gold in Switzerland and have no account there (see the section on reporting require-ments). Remember, though, you are running a risk with a claim account that you do not run with a regular custodial account. If the bank fails it is not clear who owns the gold; if it is decided the bank owns the gold the creditors could get your gold.

Having chosen how to store your gold all you have to do is buy it. There is usually a minimum purchase requirement of about 32 ounces (1 kilo). There is a brokerage charge of approximately 1/2% on purchase and sales. If you do make a sale the gold will be sold in the currency you bought it with, and your current account in that currency credited unless you leave specific instructions to the contrary. If you take physical delivery of the gold there is no additional charge above the 1/2% brokerage commission.

Forward Contracts

If you purchase forward contracts with your bank you will be required to put up a security deposit as a guarantee that you will live up to the contract on the delivery date. This security deposit is about 20% of the face value of the futures contract. Most all of the future contracts that Swiss banks trade are done on the New York Comex since that is where the most active futures market is. Each contract on the Comex is for 100 ounces. The brokerage charges at your Swiss bank for forward contracts are usually between 30 and 50% higher than those charges of the New York brokers.

Margin Accounts in Gold

This will be discussed in a later section.

Gold Coins (Bullion and Numismatic)

The procedure for buying, selling, and storing coins is the same as that for gold bullion. Storage charges are the same and gold coins are almost always held in a segregated acount. There is no direct brokerage charge but the spread between buy and sell is considerably larger than on the spot gold price. Banks deal in all the major bullion coins: Krugerrands (1 ounce), Mexican 50-peso (1.2053 ounces), Austrian 100 Krone (.9886 ounces) and the Hungarian Krone (.9886 ounces). The Swiss banks also deal in gold coins with numismatic value like the U.S. eagle and double eagle, the Swiss Vreneli, and French Napoleon. If you have a particular interest in numismatic pieces I suggest you visit the Monetarium at Credit Swiss or the numismatic department on the fourth floor of Bank Leu, both are noted worldwide for their numismatic expertise.

Gold Options

Early in 1976 Valeurs White Weld in Geneva began making a market in Gold Options. Valeurs White Weld is owned by the Credit Swiss First Boston group.

A call option gives the holder the right to purchase 5 kilos of 999.9 fine gold at any time up to a specified maturity date at a predetermined price (striking price). By buying a gold option you limit your risk. You know you can not lose more than the price of the option paid. You also have the advantage of leverage as you do not have to put up the full price of the gold. Let us take an example:

Let us say gold is trading at $248/ounce and the option for six months ahead (you can choose an option which expires in three, six or nine months) has a striking price of $266/ounce. The striking price is the price which the holder of the option (always for 5 kilos per option) will have to pay to the seller of the option if he wants to take delivery of the gold. There is also the option premium, this is the price you would have to pay the seller to acquire the right of option. This premium is subject to the forces of supply and demand. In our example let us say the option premium is $20.00 per ounce. That means the option purchaser pays 160.7537 (numbers of ounces in 5 kilos) times $20.00 equals $3,215.07. You will also have to add to this the commission charges of the bank which are at present about $40.00 per contract on both the buy and sell side.

Let us assume four months later the spot price of gold is $290/ounce. The option which is still good for another two months may now be worth $30.00 per ounce. You would now be in a position to resell the option for $4,822.61, which would be a gain of 50% on your original investment.

Of course if you wanted to you could also take physical delivery of the gold when the option expired but there would be no practical reason to do so so long as the options were selling for more than the difference between the market price of gold and the striking price.

As you can see if all goes well you can make substantial profits with little risk and little capital outlay.

On the other hand the risks are substantial too. If the market is not moving up you lose your investment. If instead you had actually bought the gold you would still have it and as long as the spot price did not go down you would not have lost anything.

For those who sell or write the options they face unlimited risk on the upside as the price of bullion moves above the striking price. The advantages of selling an option are protection against a downtrend in the price of gold and a way to earn income when the price of gold is holding steady.

If you do decide to trade options be sure you understand the mechanics of the market first. I would not go into the market in a big way; compared to the spot market the market in options is very small. Perhaps one of the best uses for gold options is hedging a short sale in the futures market.
You limit your upside risk should the price of gold go up. By buying an option you establish a maximum price that you would have to pay for the bullion in order to satisfy your short sale.

At present active option trading can only be executed through a Swiss bank as regulations in the U.S. prohibit such option trading. Approval is pending however to allow Valeurs White Weld to trade in the U.S.

Mocatta Metals in New York does some business in gold options but through Mocatta you can only purchase an option, not sell one, and at last check the premiums were quite a bit higher than those on options in Switzerland.

Paradeplatz—Zürich

CHAPTER 15

Silver and Other Precious Metal Accounts

Just as is the case for gold the spot markets for silver, platinum and palladium are very active in Switzerland. The metals are stored in Switzerland and the safekeeping fees are the same as noted before, about 1.50 Swiss francs per 1,000.00 Swiss frances of market value computed quarterly. The brokerage commission varies from between 1/4 to 1% for each side of a trade. The minimum investment is usually around 5,000.00 Swiss francs, though such limitations and conditions vary quite a bit from bank to bank.

There is also a major difference between taking delivery of gold versus other precious metals in Switzerland. The Federal authorities have imposed a 5.6% turnover tax on all metal purchases and sales (apart from gold). This need not concern most clients because the banks which trade precious metals keep a large part of their silver, platinum and palladium holdings in the duty free transit zone at the airport. So long as you do not actually take delivery of, for example, your silver holdings, then the tax can be circumvented by keeping the metal stored at the transit zone.

It is also possible to purchase silver coins through some Swiss banks. You must realize though that the market for bags of silver coins is in the U.S. Your Swiss bank will trade these bags in New York under its name. The physical bag remains in storage in New York. If you trade silver bags it will cost you more to do it through Switzerland than through a broker in New York and there is no advantage apart from anonymity. You will find that only banks that specialize in a North American clientele will offer such silver coin custodial accounts.

To better understand the system by which you would open and deal in a precious metals account we shall follow through a typical example.

Mr. Miller is an American who believes an investment in silver would be in his interest at this time. He has the option of doing this is several ways:

1. He can buy shares in a silver mining company.
2. He can purchase silver coins.
3. He can buy silver bars.
4. He can purchase silver jewelry.
5. He can purchase silver for forward delivery either through the futures or the options market.

He also has a number of alternatives to finance these purchases:

1. He can make his purchase outright paying full value for the silver he invests in.
2. He can borrow funds to make his purchase.
3. He can purchase silver coins, silver bullion, and silver for forward delivery on margin. Buying on margin means that he only pays a portion of the total cost and the bank or broker grants him a credit on the rest using the silver as collateral. (We will discuss this in greater detail in a later section).

These then are the alternatives open to the investor. Mr. Miller does not like the idea of debt and interest costs and since he is quite liquid, decides to purchase the silver outright. His only problem is he can not decide whether to purchase silver bullion or go into the futures market. Because he values his privacy and is fearful that his government might want, one day, to seize his assets he decides to play it safe and invest through his Swiss bank.

If he invests in futures he understands that the Swiss bank will trade the futures contracts either in New York, Chicago or London. In New York and Chicago the contract size is 5,000 troy ounces of 999 fine silver. In London a minimum contract is 10,000 ounces and any odd lot amount over that will be traded, for example, 16,000 ounces. In New York or Chicago he can only trade in multiples of 5,000 ounces.

In both cases Mr. Miller will have to pay the brokerage commission of both his Swiss bank and of the dealer abroad (he does get a discount on the commission paid to the broker abroad as the trade is being effected through his Swiss bank at bank rates).

Mr. Miller could also purchase options on silver through London and to a more limited extent through New York. His Swiss bank could help him in either case.

Because he is new to all of this and as he does not have the time nor the patience to carefully monitor the fluctuations in silver prices, Mr. Miller decides it is better to start out with basics and simply buy the silver outright.

He writes to his bank and instructs it to purchase silver for him in London or New York or he may simply request that it buy silver for him and hold it at the free transit zone warehouse. We have already discussed the ways in which he can send funds to Switzerland to cover the purchase. Should there be a balance remaining after the purchase it will be credited to his current account and he can leave instructions for its further dispersal or he can simply hold it there.

Let us say that Mr. Miller, after making a small profit, decides to sell his silver holdings. Mr. Miller should include his metals account number when passing on instructions to the bank. The sales proceeds minus deductions for commission and safe keeping charges will be credited to his current account. Mr. Miller could also give such instructions over the phone but first he would have to have a contact man at the bank who could recognize his voice and secondly, most banks would require that he confirm his call by writing a letter with the same instructions (his orders will be carried out after the phone call but the bank still wants written confirmation for its records).

This was the most straightforward way Mr. Miller could have invested in silver, but as we suggested earlier another technique would have been to buy silver, or any other precious metal, stock, bond or foreign currency on margin. As this is perhaps the most popular technique among investors we shall now examine some of its aspects.

CHAPTER 16

Margin Accounts

Every prudent investor should think twice before buying on margin. In a bull market it looks great but in a declining market your financial base can literally collapse beneath you.

When you buy on margin through your Swiss bank you pay for a portion of the total cost of what you are purchasing and your bank pays for the rest. A credit charge is made to you on the amount you get from the bank. In effect you are taking a loan and offering as collateral a security, precious metal or other asset. You may even offer as collateral that which you are purchasing. The amount of margin (that is to say the value you may borrow against) varies from time to time but at present is as follows among the Swiss banks:

Type of Asset	Amount of margin offered (based on market value)
U.S. shares (must have daily quote, not OTC)	50%
Swiss quoted shares	60%
U.S. bonds	50 to 60%
Swiss bonds	70 to 80%
South African gold shares	30%
Precious metals	60%
Real estate and other	check with individual bank

Using the above numbers it would, for example, be possible for you to purchase 100,000.00 francs of gold by only putting up 40,000.00 francs. This 40,000.00 francs is known as your equity. Should the price of gold decrease and your original investment would be worth only 90,000.00 francs; then your equity would correspondingly decrease by 10,000.00 francs. Your new equity of 30,000.00 francs as compared to the market value of the gold would now be equivalent to only 33% of the market value. Since the bank only offers margin up to 60% you would be required to deposit another 6,000.00 francs in order to bring your equity back in line at 40%. This process of requiring you to increase your equity in order to bring your margin back in line is known as a margin call. Should you not meet the margin call for any reason a portion of your holdings will be sold so as to bring your margin back in line.

If you indicate to the bank that you want to make a purchase on margin they will open a separate margin account in your name. It is the same for all practical purposes as having been granted a loan by the bank. The interest charges at present are around 6%/annum for Swiss francs and 13%/annum for U.S. dollars. These rates are reviewed monthly and are a function of market interest rates as well as of the balances held by the bank in the margin accounts.

If you buy on margin and offer as collateral something other than that when you are purchasing, these assets must be placed in safekeeping with the bank that is extending you the margin. In either case, that is whether you margin other holdings or margin that which you are purchasing, it is necessary to sign a general declaration of pledge with the bank. If you read the declaration you will notice you are agreeing to give the bank full claim to your margined assets, and that the bank can dispose of the collateral *even* if the full claim is not yet due. As we already noted this will be the case either when you do not answer your margin call or are unable to because of financial reasons. (See p. 182)

Let us go back once more to our Mr. Miller to better understand how this process works. Let us say he had bought 5,000 ounces of silver outright which was being held at the free transit warehouse at Kloten airport in Zürich. The market value of the 5,000 ounces is we shall say US$40,000.00. Now Mr. Miller has had time to study the situation a little better and foresees an upsurge in the silver price but he does not want to liquidate any of his other assets; yet, he would like to own more silver. He can do this by leveraging his silver holdings and purchasing more silver on margin. Sixty percent of $40,000. gives him $24,000. with which he can purchase 3,000 additional ounces at $8/ounce. He can, however, margin the silver he purchases with the $24,500, also at 60%. If he decides to margin all his silver holdings he will have $100,000. worth of silver or 12,500 ounces at an initial cost of $40,000. He will also have a margin account and will be paying interest on the $60,000.00 margin granted him by the bank. Additionally he will have the extra storage cost and the commission charges for the purchase of the additional 7,500 ounces.

One of two things can now happen. Mr. Miller may have guessed right and silver goes up to $8.50/ounce. He can then instruct his bank to sell his holdings in account No. 000XYZ. With the proceeds he pays back the margin, covers the interest, commission and storage charges. Then, depending upon which tax bracket he is in, he enjoys the profit from what was effectively a $100,000.00 investment although he only put up $40,000.00.

Mr. Miller may also have guessed wrong. A year goes by and Mr. Miller has paid $7,800.00 in interest alone and the price of silver has not moved.

Suddenly it moves—down. When Mr. Miller's equity falls to about 32% the bank will make a margin call. Let us say silver slipped to $7/ounce. Mr. Miller then has 12,500 ounces at $7/ounce or $87,500.00 for which his equity is $27,500.00 or about 31% on the market value. The bank will at this point issue a margin call. The call may be sent either by cable or by registered mail. If Mr. Miller responds, it is best that he do so by cable if possible. In his reply he should once again include his account number and if he is going to meet the call, he should indicate when and how he is going to forward the funds needed to the bank.

In this particular case the margin call for Mr. Miller will be for $7,500.00 which would bring his equity back up to 40% of the market value of the silver. The bank will accept either cash or U.S. Treasury Bills to meet the margin call. If the funds promised by Mr. Miller do not arrive within two weeks after the margin call date (2 weeks after the margin call was dispatched) the bank will sell the required amount of the client's holdings to meet the call. If no reply at all were received from Mr. Miller within a week or so of the margin call, then it is assumed by the bank that he wants them to sell the required amount of his holdings to meet the call.

Assuming Mr. Miller does not meet the call, he has held his silver for one year and has lost a minimum of 50% on his equity while also suffering an additional 11% depreciation in his silver holdings. During the same period, had he owned the silver outright, he would have suffered only a 12.5% loss in comparison.

There are additional risks which Mr. Miller may also have to

General Declaration of Pledge

The undersigned _____

residing in _____

does/do give   Bank NB   as collateral security on all present or future claims held by

said Bank against _____

regardless of the legal basis from which such claims arise (e.g. present or future loans, bills of exchange, stock exchange business), including any due or current interests, commissions and cost of proceedings: – all his/her/their securities at present or hereafter in safekeeping with the Bank or otherwise in the Bank's possession or deposited elsewhere in the Bank's name, and also all his/her/their credit balances with said Bank (including credit balances in foreign currencies or the equivalent thereof in Swiss francs), and also claims, cash bank notes and other rights and values including all outstanding and current preference and subsidiary rights relating thereto (interests, dividends, etc. – in case of mortgage titles pursuant to Sec. 818 of the Swiss Civil Code), and does/do assign all such items to said Bank for collateral purposes.

In the event of collaterals being exchanged, the substituted items shall immediately become operative as collaterals.

Also, the undersigned undertake(s), if directly any decrease in value has occurred or is imminent in the Bank's opinion, at any time at the Bank's option either to improve the collaterals in a manner thought fit by the Bank, or to effect the payment required. If such request by the Bank, which is to be mailed by registered letter to the last-known address of the Pledgor, fails to be duly answered within the time allowed, or if the Pledgor falls in default otherwise, the Bank shall be at liberty to dispose freely of the collaterals (if possible at the stock exchange), or to institute action either for distraint or bankruptcy or sale of collaterals, even if the claim is not yet due.

The Bank will use its best endeavours to safeguard the right arising from the collaterals (supervision of drawings, payments, amortizations, petitions, etc.), but without assuming any liability whatsoever.

The Bank is entitled, but not bound, to give notice for, and to collect pledged titles, bills of exchange, claims, etc., and also to collect interests, dividends, etc., and to represent shares at the General Meeting.

The relationship between the Bank and the Pledgor shall be governed in its entirety by Swiss law. The place of performance shall be the domicile of   Bank NB in Switzerland.

Bank NB is explicitly entitled to hand pledges which are entrusted to them over to third persons as a pawn.

In the event of any dispute arising hereunder, the Pledgor undertakes, at the request of the Bank, to recognize the place of jurisdiction of the Bank and to establish his domicile at that place for the purpose.

_____, the _____, 19_____

The Pledgor: _____

face. It is possible that the price of silver may drop so fast that he could miss the margin calls or not be able to keep up and lose a large part of his equity. This was the case for many a silver investor about 10 years ago when silver took a sudden plunge.

There is also an exchange rate risk inherent in any borrowings. Let us say Mr. Miller margins his original silver purchase against Swiss francs. With the Swiss francs he purchases gold bullion. After six months the price of gold denominated in Swiss francs is still about the same as when he bought the gold, but meanwhile the Swiss franc has appreciated 25% against the dollar. To repay the Swiss franc loan, Mr. Miller will now have to pay 25% more dollars and meanwhile his Swiss franc investment will have earned no income.

Mr. Miller may have preferred borrowing Swiss francs because the interest charges on Swiss franc borrowings were lower. Do not be fooled into thinking that just because the Swiss franc loans have a low interest charge that they are a "better deal." The interest differential between the price for Swiss franc or U.S. dollar loans reflects the anticipated appreciation of one currency vis-à-vis the other in the coming year. Should there be an appreciation of the currency you are borrowing your loss could not only offset the interest rate differential but also lead into a bigger loss as well.

CHAPTER 17

Instructions to Your Swiss Bank

There are certain rules and some basic vocabulary terms with which you should be acquainted while doing business with your Swiss bank.

Assuming that you openly communicate with your bank, that is, that you are not concerned with preserving your privacy, then there are several expedient procedures that you should observe:

1. In all correspondence with the bank remember to always give the relevant account number. All accounts have individual numbers for each account; this is for organizational reasons. Therefore,if you have a current account, a safekeeping gold account and a margin account you will have a separate designation for each, for example: current account: 816.773.M; margin account: 816.773G; safekeeping gold: 816.773.G.03. The term "numbered account" is, as previously explained, for internal security reasons and would in this example mean that 816.773 would refer to another number in the records say, XX352,rather than to a person's name.

2. Always confirm in writing any transaction or instruction you make over the phone. Repeat the instruction or transaction in your letter and give the date of the telephone conversation.

3. Make copies of all letters you send the bank, for your own records and to insure that the bank executes your instructions correctly.

4. Have a contact at the bank and if there are any problems call him.

If you are keeping your account secret then, of course, you want to avoid all the above. Never accept any mail from the bank; never send the bank any correspondence except perhaps through a safe third party; do not have a discussion with your banker over the phone. Most international calls made from nearly anywhere in the world can be traced and are often taped.

If you want to keep your account secret, do it through a third party or visit the bank yourself if necessary.

Vocabulary:

There are certain words which are ubiquitously used in investment banking and you should be able to make use of them and their concepts in your investing too:

Limit order: "Dear Bank NB:I would like to place a limit order to buy 5,000 ounces of gold at $285/ounce." A limit order instructs the bank to buy or sell only at a specified price, or better. A "limit order to buy" means that in the above example the bank will buy the gold at $285/ounce or any price below that. If the above instructions were a "limit order to sell" then the bank would sell your 5,000 ounces of gold at $285/ounce or any price higher (e.g. $287/ounce). (Note: Not all banks will accept limit orders.) .

Stop loss: "Dear Bank NB: I would like to place a stop loss at $15.80 on my 2,000 shares of GAP account number 02345.L.2". A stop loss is probably the most important type of standing order and has widespread practical usage. A stop loss can be issued for precious metals, securities and currencies. A stop loss (or stop sell) is placed a certain percentage or certain number of points below the market price and is there to protect you if there is a fall in the market. A stop loss is to protect you in case the market falls while you are not looking.

Using our GAP example let us say you purchased GAP at $15/share and the market is now at $16.50. You are unsure as to how the situation will further develop but have a feeling that GAP should go up in price before it goes down. Just in case you are wrong, you place a stop loss at $15.80/share; this way at least you will preserve some of your profit should the stock start to go down in price.

There is also something known as the stop buy order, which is a stop loss order for someone with a short position. The stop buy order is placed several points above the price where you have your position. If the market should go up, instead of down as you had hoped, then you will automatically be stopped out of the market before you can lose more money.

In either case of using the stop loss order technique you can at any time adjust your stop loss to follow the market. Should the market respond as you had hoped, then you will probably want to raise your stop loss order on a long position or correspondingly lower it if you are short.

Something you will want to pay particular attention to when giving your bank any such type of standing order is that all such advance buy/sell orders, limit orders, or stop loss orders expire automatically after 60 days from date of receipt unless renewed by the client. Because of the difficulty in monitoring such orders some banks may not even accept them for smaller accounts. If you plan on doing any speculative trading through your Swiss bank you might want to first make sure the bank accepts such orders, and under what conditions.

CHAPTER 18

Swiss Stock Market Transactions

There are several stock markets in Switzerland, the most important being the one located in Zürich. All the major banks are represented at the exchange and there is quite heavy trading in the over 2,200 stocks quoted there. All trading is done in the name of the bank which is acting as broker on the exchange. In the first quarter of 1979 the volume averaged about 10 thousand million Swiss francs per month on the Zürich exchange.

The system used in the Swiss exchanges to make trades is quite different from that known in other parts of the world. The stock exchange system used in Zürich is commonly called "a la criee". The way it is organized there are three rings about which the brokers are assembled. One of the rings is for trading bonds and the other two for domestic and foreign stocks. The market is officially open from 10:00 to 12:30 a.m. each work day. Trading not done between those hours is completed in regular over the counter fashion between the banks.

If you were to visit the exchange you would see several officials of the exchange seated in the middle of each of the rings. These officials keep track of and regulate the trading. One of them will "cry" out the name of the bond or stock to be traded and each of the brokers declares what position he wishes to take. Other brokers try to match his bid or ask and a price is negotiated. After bids and offers are presented and negotiated the price and number of shares traded are noted by another one of the officials. He also notes the appropriate allocation among the brokers involved in the transaction. When trading is completed in one share a new one is called out and the dealing continues. Once trading on a share is completed the brokers can not go back to it until the next time its name comes up again. So long as most of the trading is limited to several hundred different stocks and bonds this system can proceed efficiently. As the size of the market grows, however, some changes may have to be made for reasons of expediency. A sub-committee of the exchange commission is now examining other possibilities for trading, but if any changes are to be made they are probably still a long way off.

The advantages to a foreigner of trading on the Zürich exchange are that he can also trade shares of many foreign corporations right in Zürich. Trading in Zürich protects you further from foreign government interference and in general, you can save on brokerage charges and taxes by trading directly in Zürich.

Presently shares of some 70 U.S. firms as well as 128 German, 10 English, 5 Canadian and 8 South African firms are traded in Zürich. In total nearly 400 bonds and 150 stocks of 34 different countries are quoted on the Zürich exchange.

Dividends paid by non—Swiss companies are not subject to the Swiss withholding tax although they may be subject to taxes in the country of origin.

It is said that another advantage of trading on the Swiss exchanges is that brokerage fees and other charges make for cheaper trading here than elsewhere in the world. It is difficult to compare fee structures while they are based on widely differing criteria among the various countries. Using an example, though, in which we compare charges for buying 10 or 100 shares respectfully of company BB's stock which is quoted at 151.00 francs in Zürich we come up with the following costs.[1]

Place traded	Brokerage fee and local tax	
	for 10 shares	*for 100 shares*
	in Swiss francs	
Zürich	11.80	111.90
New York	41.20	190.90
Frankfurt	20.40	203.80
Amsterdam	16.90	169.10
Paris	16.90	169.60
London	22.60	226.30

From this we would deduce that Zürich is considerably cheaper than other places. To a large degree that is true.

Remember however, that the exchange rate risk can quickly overshadow this savings. Furthermore, for any substantial trading you will find that the competitiveness and volume of the Zürich market is no match for New York.

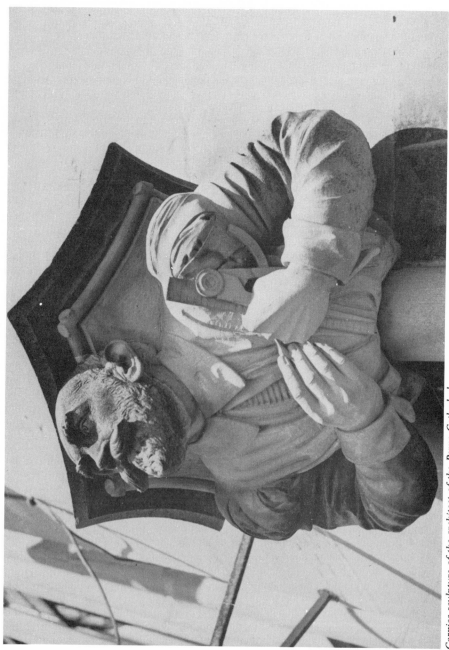

Cornice sculpture of the architect of the Berne Cathedral.

CHAPTER 19

Foreign Exchange Transactions

One of the factors that makes Switzerland so important as a financial center is the strength of the Swiss franc. The popularity of investing in Swiss francs has turned the franc into a fairly volatile commodity much like gold or wheat. No matter how the Swiss government may try to counter this trend it will continue so long as Switzerland is able to maintain an inflation rate below that of other major industrialized countries.

If you do business in or through Switzerland you may be affected by these variations. You must always be careful to think about what currencies your assets are denominated in. Depending on how spread out your assets are and how stable the currencies you hold are you will be influenced in varying degrees by currency fluctuations.

These days the best way to look at currencies is to simply think of them as investments and analyze them much in the same way that you would analyze a stock or bond. Technical and fundamental analyses as well as basic economic knowledge are all important. Your Swiss banker will have had considerable experience in foreign currency dealings and in times of doubt he is another good source to turn to.

Without doubt in times of uncertainty it it best to diversify. As long as your assets are not denominated all in one currency you avoid having all your eggs in one basket. The prudent investor will expose himself to as little exchange rate risk as possible.

If you should decide to make an investment in something denominated in a foreign currency, remember you are making in effect two investments. If you buy 12 kilos of gold for 200,000.00 Swiss francs do not expect gold to go up vis à vis the Swiss franc just because you expected gold to go up versus the dollar. The demand for gold may be derived from the same demand as that for the Swiss franc and they may be mutually inclusive alternatives in the market.

The all-around best tack to take is to keep your investing simple and to the point.

A common problem that arises between banks and their customers is a misunderstanding over exchange rates. Many customers question the validity of their banks' quotations. Customers often feel the bank is trying to make money on them by exchanging their money at poor rates. In fact, although you may be able to catch a bank whose exchange rate is out of line, that will seldom be the case. If it does occur, it is most probably because of an error rather than an intentional revision. Every morning and afternoon the Swiss banks, hotels and shops fix their exchange rates at the same level for their customers. These rates are fixed by convention and fairly strictly adhered to.

For financial transactions your bank may give you a more favourable rate if you are a well known client and have a large transaction.

If you want to monitor exchange rate differences be sure you monitor from the right source. For example, if you see rates quoted on the financial page of your newspaper do not assume that these rates would apply to you as a bank customer. In all likelihood the rates quoted on the financial pages of a newspaper are interbank rates. If you were trading in tens of millions of Swiss francs you might be able to get such rates, otherwise probably not.

In Switzerland foreign exchange rates between banks are all quoted in terms of the dollar. If you see a quote of 1.648/1.649 for Swiss francs then the first rate is the buying rate for the dollar or the selling rate for the Swiss franc. The second is the selling rate for the dollar or the buying rate for the Swiss franc. We can also divide the rates above into one dollar to get the value of one Swiss franc in dollars in this case .6064/.6068 (Note: We reverse buy and sell rates because we are now not comparing the buying and selling rate for the dollar but the buying and selling rate for Swiss francs).

One set of calculations all international investors should be acquainted with is figuring cross rates. This is necessary for doing

THE MONTHLY PERCENTAGE CHANGE IN THE EXCHANGE RATE OF MAJOR CURRENCIES AGAINST THE U.S. DOLLAR BEGINNING WITH THE AVERAGE EXCHANGE RATE FOR 1974:

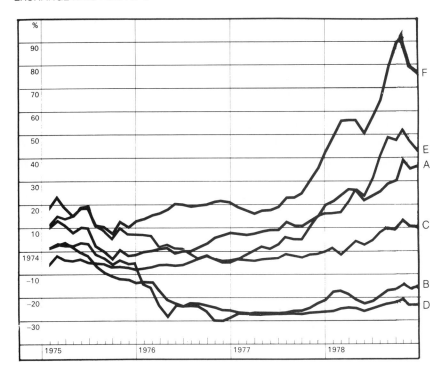

A = GERMAN MARK   D = ITALIAN LIRE
B = ENGLISH POUND   E = JAPANESE YEN
C = FRENCH FRANC   F = SWISS FRANC

Source: Swiss National Bank Annual Report 1978

business in currencies other than the dollar. We will follow through an example for illustrative purposes.

Let us say you want to buy Japanese Yen against some of the Swiss francs you now have with your bank. Let us say the rates on the day this transaction occurs are as follows:

	Buying	**Selling**
$/Yen	208.10	208.40
$/SF	1.648	1.649

The bank will buy the Yen against dollars from the Nippon bank at their buying rate for dollars (here 208.10). Likewise to get these dollars your bank will have to sell your Swiss francs to another bank at their selling rate for dollars (1.649). (The bank may also be able to buy the Yen and/or sell the Swiss francs to themselves if they have a position in these currencies).

The rate then for Yen in terms of Swiss francs is:

1.649 (to sell Swiss francs against dollars)=.0079 SF/Yen
208.10 (to buy Yen against dollars)

If you exchanged 25,000.00 Swiss francs then this would give you:

.0079 SF/Yen = 1/.0079   Yen/SF = 126.58
25,000.00 Swiss francs times 126.58 Yen/SF = 3,164,500 Yen.

Now this is the price the bank had to pay for the Yen, so they will add a little margin to their cost when they send you your statement.

It is this type of transaction that occurs whenever there is an exchange between two currencies. Remember the basis for the transaction is always the dollar. It will be easier for you to understand your bank statement if you keep that in mind.

CHAPTER 20

Restrictions and Taxes for Foreign Account Holders

In a previous section we discussed in general fashion the implications of restrictions imposed by the National Bank. As of August 1979 several of these restrictions were amended. Below, the restrictions that could affect you as a foreign account holder are summarized. Remember these rules apply to those who are about to open an account as well as those who already have an account in a Swiss bank. (These restrictions apply only to Swiss franc deposits.)

1. Purchase of Swiss franc forward contracts are limited under the same guidelines as were discussed on page 102.
2. New rules now allow you to hold up to 200,000 Swiss francs without any interest penalty. These 200,000 francs must be divided among accounts serving different purposes.
   a. You may have up to 100,000 Swiss francs in an interest bearing account (e.g. deposit or savings accounts; time deposits are still not allowed).
   b. You may have up to another 100,000 Swiss francs in a non-interest bearing account (e.g. current account).
3. If you had an account in your Swiss bank before October 31, 1974, the balance you had before that date, as long as it is below 5 million francs, remains commission free (but you can earn interest on only 100,000 francs of that amount).
4. If you have more than 100,000 Swiss francs in either of the accounts described in 2 above (or more than 5,100,000 Swiss francs if you have continually maintained an account since before October 31, 1974) then the balance over those limitations is subject to a negative 2.5% commission or negative interest tax per quarter.

5. Under the new rules, if interest earned on your account brings your balance over 100,000 Swiss francs it is then subject to the negative 2.5% interest charge. So if you have an account of 100,000 Swiss francs earning interest be sure to instruct the bank to transfer your interest into another currency account when it comes due.

6. Each member of a family who is no longer a minor (age 21) can qualify to open a 100,000 interest earning and a 100,000 non-interest earning Swiss franc account. Note these limitations apply to accounts at each bank. A family of two could hold 1.2 million Swiss francs commission free, half of it earning interest, by together having accounts in three different banks.

7. It is no longer permissible for a bank to hold Swiss franc banknotes or cashiers checks in a safekeeping account as an entity separate from your other accounts. You can, however, give the bank a sealed envelope to hold without divulging the contents.

8. There are no restrictions on the import of currencies into Switzerland nor on export of Swiss franc banknotes. Restrictions on purchase of marketed Swiss bonds and stocks have been removed.

Taxes

There are no capital gain taxes in Switzerland. The tax which foreign account holders do have to worry about in Switzerland is withholding tax. The Swiss withholding tax applies to dividends and also to interest earned on bank balances. The withholding tax rate is 35% but in many cases all or part of this is recoverable if the country in which you reside has a double taxation agreement with Switzerland. The chart on   page 200   illustrates the relief available to account holders who are subject to the withholding tax.

If we look at this chart and use the U.S. as an example, let us say that an account holder earns 10,000 U.S. dollars interest over a one year period. This means that the bank will withhold 3,500 dollars for the Swiss government. On the account holder's bank balance at year end he will be given a net credit of 6,500 dollars interest income. If the account holder wishes to reclaim part of this tax he can do so by filling out the tax form R82 which is available from his Swiss bank. Filling out this form entitles the account holder to reclaim 6/7 of the tax withheld by the Swiss. In this example, then, the Swiss tax authorities will pay into his account 3,000 dollars, making his net tax 500 dollars or 5%.

The Swiss withholding tax does not apply to all investments in Switzerland. Interest paid on government bonds, and bonds of certain other borrowers, for example, are exempt from the withholding tax. Further exemptions are certificates of deposit and funds earning interest through a fiduciary deposit. Fiduciary deposits are not exempt from the withholding tax if the account holder has not signed a fiduciary agreement with his bank stating that the funds are being held outside of Switzerland. Earnings from precious metal holdings are, of course, exempt from the withholding tax as they represent capital gains.

Swiss Taxes Withheld for Residents of Other Countries

Country	Dividends			Interest[1]		
	Normal Rate	Relief[2]	Net Tax[3]	Normal Rate	Relief[2]	Net Tax[3]
Australia*	35%	0%	35%	35%	0%	35%
Austria	35	30	5	35	30	5
Belgium*	35	0	35	35	0	35
Canada	35	20	15	35	20[4]	15[4]
France[5]	35	30[6]	5[6]	35	25	16
Germany[7]	35	20	15	35	35	0
Great Britain	35	20	15	35	35	0
minimum 25% owner	35	30	5	—	—	—
Italy*[8]	35	0	35	35	0	35
Japan	35	20	15	35	25	10
minimum 25% owner	35	25	10	—	—	—
Netherlands	35	20	15	35	30	5
minimum 25% owner	35	35	0	—	—	—
South Africa	35	27.5	7.5	35	0[9]	35[9]
USA	35	20	15	35	30	5
minimum 95% owner	35	30[10]	5[10]	—	—	—

*Countries with which Switzerland has concluded no double taxation agreement.

[1]Including interest on bank balances, savings accounts, etc.

[2]Procedure: generally, retrospective refund.

[3]In most countries, the net tax can be credited against local income tax. Exceptions include Finland, Italy, Norway.

[4]Interest paid on government bonds and certain other bonds is granted relief from the 35% withholding tax.

[5]Limitations on claims for benefits are similar to those applying to Swiss companies with pre-dominant foreign control.

[6]If at least 20% ownership, the tax relief is 20% (net tax 15%) unless shares of one of the companies is publicly traded.

[7]For companies and foundations limitations are similar to footnote 6.

[8]Treaty agreement pending. Withholding tax would be reduced to 15% on dividends and 12½% on interest.

[9]No relief as long as no tax is imposed on foreign interest paid to South African creditors.

[10]The reduction to 5% is only granted in extraordinary cases.

Switzerland - United States Income Tax Convention signed May 24, 1951 (Articles VI and VII)

File Number
SR - R 82 -

R 82   Claim to refund of Swiss tax

withheld at source on dividends and interest derived from sources within Switzerland

For claimant: Retain this copy for your file while claim is pending. Do not forward it with original and duplicate to Switzerland.

Form for use by: (a) Individuals resident in the United States (other than Swiss citizens who are not also citizens of the United States (b) United States corporations (c) other United States entities.

Filing of claim: This form, duly completed and signed before a notary public of the United States, must be sent (duplicate unseparated) to the Federal Tax Administration of Switzerland, Bundesgasse 32, CH - 3003 Berne, Switzerland. **It must be accompanied by suitable evidence of deduction of Swiss tax withheld at source, such as certificates of deduction, signed bank vouchers or credit slips, etc.;** these documents (certificates of deduction excepted) will be returned to the claimant. If the claimant, at the time of claiming, is outside the United States, the declaration may be made before a United States consular officer.

Time of filing: This form may be filed on or after July 1 or January 1 next following upon the date payable of the income, but **not later than December 31 of the third** year following upon the calendar year in which the income became payable.

I. Claimant

Name in full: ....
(Block letters)

Full residential address: ....

II. Questions to be answered by the claimant

On the date(s) set out in column 5 on the back hereof:

1. were you beneficially entitled to the income specified on the back hereof?

2. were you engaged in trade or business in Switzerland through a permanent establishment situated therein? ....

3. a) were you an individual resident in the United States? ....   b) were you an individual resident in Switzerland? ....

c) were you a citizen of the United States? ....   d) were you a citizen of Switzerland? ....

4. were you a United States corporation? .... (indicate State of incorporation) ....

5. were you a United States entity (other than a corporation)? .... (give full details of claimant and of all persons concerned, including their residence, wherever situated, and their proportionate shares under observations on the back hereof)

III. Further requirements

6. Claimant's last United States income tax return, relating to the year .... was filed with the Internal Revenue Service Center at

....

Claimant's Taxpayer Identifying Number / Social Security Account No: ....

7. The claimant has not filed or caused to be filed any other claim for refund of Swiss tax in respect of items of income listed on the back hereof and has no knowledge of any other person or persons having claimed or caused to be claimed a refund of Swiss tax in respect of such income

8. The claimant will furnish additional information and/or documentary evidence if called upon to do so by the Federal Tax Administration of Switzerland

IV. Claim

9. The claimant therefore claims refund of Swiss tax amounting to Swiss Fr. .... as set out on the back hereof which amount

is to be paid for his account to the following bank: ....

.... Account number: ....
(Remittance by check is only made if claimant has no bank account)

V. Declaration

I/We hereby solemnly declare, under the penalties of perjury, that the statements made by me/us in the present claim, including the data listed on the reverse side hereof, are correct and true to the best of my/our knowledge and belief.

....
Signature of claimant or declarant(s)

If signed by persons other than the claimant, their full names, residential addresses and capacity must be added hereafter:

....

....

Declared at ....

this .... day of .... 19 ......

(Seal)

before me ....
(Signature and title of notary public or consular officer)

Address ....

R 82 3. 77 49211

Back of Form R 82

SCHEDULE of income taxed at source, in respect of which refund of Swiss tax is claimed

Specification of income entitled to tax refund at the rate of
20 %: Dividends from Swiss corporations and similar income
30 %: Interest on Swiss bonds and bank deposits
In column 2, state exact date of acquisition, if acquired within twelve months prior to date payable shown in column 5.
If acquired earlier, just state "prior to 19 . . ."

To be used
only for the due dates
from the January 1, 1976

Capital investment			Income taxed at source (enter **gross** amounts)			
Description of securities (stock in Swiss corporations, bonds, bank deposits, etc.) Name of debtor	Date of acquisition	Number of shares; the others total par value Fr.	Dividend per share Rate (%) of interest	Date payable of dividend, interest etc. (day, month, year)	Dividends Fr.	Interest Fr.
1	2	3	4	5	6	7

Observations
(Use separate sheets in duplicate, if necessary)

Enclosures:

Total gross amounts of income taxed

Fr. .... Fr. ....

For official use only

Claim for refund

Fr. .... Fr. ....

20 % on total of col. 6 Fr. ....

....

30 % on total of col. 7 Fr. ....

Total claim   Fr. ....

Fr. .... to be refunded

Refund made ....

Duplicate sent O. I. O. ....

R 82

CHAPTER 21

Switzerland as a Tax Haven

A tax haven is a country in which you can accumulate capital at tax rates more favorable than those found in your home country. In many ways you can consider a tax haven as a sanctuary for your money. There is nothing gimmicky about the tax havens and if properly utilized they can save a considerable amount in taxes legally.

There are several factors that must be considered when choosing a tax haven. The first essential is, not surprisingly, that the country have tax laws favorable to you and your situation. What you will be looking for as a businessman and investor is low income and capital taxes, favorable conditions for incorporation and for your personal fortune low inheritance taxes. The other factors you should look for in a tax haven are privacy, security and stability. It will not do you any good to be paying no taxes and have the threat of nationalization of your assets hanging over you. Furthermore, in the case of a tax haven, as for a bank account, the less attention that is drawn to it the better.

Switzerland, though not an ideal tax haven, meets the criteria in general quite well. The conditions for taxation vary from canton have to canton in the confederation. Some cantons have deliberately written their tax law in such a way as to attract foreign companies. In the canton of Zug, for example, if you look down a list of holding companies incorporated there, it reads like a Who's Who of major multinational firms.

Income taxes vary among the cantons from about 3% to 30%. Inheritance taxes are practically non-existent or fairly easily circumvented. As far as security, privacy and stability are concerned, we have probably written enough about that already. Banking secrecy is here to stay and we discussed the legal position of the account holder vis-à-vis his bank.

In the last chapter we discussed the taxes and restrictions which a foreign account holder is liable for in Switzerland. Through your Swiss bank account you should be able to earn a certain amount of tax free capital profit and some tax free income from a variety of investments. This is for someone who has put a part of their assets to the side for savings and investment purposes. If, however, you want to keep your money alive in Switzerland in a commercial sense, and if you plan on repatriating some of these funds, then you must investigate the conditions for forming a Swiss corporation.

Formation of Companies in Switzerland

In general, the laws governing the formation of companies in Switzerland are like those to be found in the U.K. or the U.S. The structure of the corporations is also similar to those found in these countries. There are basically some seven different forms a firm can take under the law. These are briefly examined below:

Einfache Gesellschaft: (Association): The law (Code of Obligation, henceforth referred to as "OR" Article 530, paragraph 1) defines this as a collective organized to fulfill a business or community endeavour. Generally such an association is not registered in the Handelsregister (Commercial Register). It is not recognized as a legal personality and carries no proper firm name.

Kollektivgesellschaft: (General Partnership): This is an association made up of two or more individuals. Unlike with the einfache Gesellschaft the individuals here cannot be of a solely legal nature; they must be natural persons. The purpose of the association is "to operate a trading, industrial or other commercial enterprise in the firm's name" (OR 552, paragraph 1). The partners have unlimited liability to the creditors of such an organization.

Legally the firm is not recognized as a corporate body. As an association though it can acquire rights and incur liabilities, take legal action and be sued.

Creation of such a partnership is effected through a written contract and the partnership must be entered in the commercial register.

Kommanditgesellschaft: (Limited Partnership):
This is similar to a general partnership with the difference that at least one of the partners is fully liable for the debts and obligations of the firm, and the liability of the remaining partners is limited to a fixed contribution (OR 594).

Legal creation of such a partnership also follows the guidelines set forth for the general partnership. When the firm's name appears in the Commercial Register it is followed by the description "& Co." The extent of the limited liability must also be made public.

Aktiengesellschaft: (Corporation): This "corporation" is probably best suited to meet the requirements of foreign businesses. Such a corporation exists under its own firm name and in its by-laws must stipulate its object or business purpose, its internal organization, its capitalization and the procedure for calling shareholders' meetings. Its capital is divided into shares and its liabilities are covered exclusively by its assets (OR620).

The nominal share capital is fixed at a minimum of 50,000.00 Swiss francs, of which at least 20,000.00 francs must be paid in at the time of incorporation. The company's capital may be raised through the acquisition of assets other than money; if this is the case, however, there are certain rules of procedure and requirements that must be met. You must refer to the specific law for different cases.

Share certificates may be issued either to bearer or registered in the name of the owner. Bearer shares can only be offered after the entire nominal share capital has been paid in. It is possible to restrict transferability of registered shares in the corporation's by-laws. Share certificates must have a par value of not less than 200.00 Swiss francs per share. There is no issuing of "no par value" shares under Swiss law.

The organization of the corporation: At least three prospective shareholders are required for formation of a corporation. There are no legal restrictions as to the nationality of the shareholders. However, you should realize that in the name of defending the Swiss franc there are times when the government may forbid or require that foreigners get approval before they can participate in existing companies. This is, for example, now the case with realty companies.

Strolling through the Old Town of Zürich, visitors may enjoy a game of chess on the Lindenhof.

It is possible for an investor to remain anonymous by having a trustee subscribe on his behalf. This is not true in all instances, however, and again you would have to seek legal counsel in the particular instance to determine whether or not this were possible.

The general organization of the corporation is comprised of the shareholders, the board of directors, and the auditors. Their respective functions are the same as those of corresponding entities in the U.S., Canada, and the U.K.

A majority of the Board must be made up of Swiss citizens living in Switzerland. Each member of the Board must own at least one share of the share capital. You can arrange it through a Swiss attorney that he represent you on the Board. In this way you can retain control despite having to take Swiss Board members.

Executive personnel can be foreign nationals. They require a permit from the Swiss immigration officials in order to take up residency in Switzerland. The facility with which such personnel can be brought into Switzerland varies with the type of work and the quota asigned by the federal authorities in that particular field.

The cost of forming a Swiss corporation, all inclusive, is about 5,000.00 Swiss francs. It may also be possible to "pick up" a dormant company for a somewhat smaller fee. Whether this is possible or not depends on what your needs are and what is available. You can ask your banker for information on this.

It is also possible to transfer the domicile of a foreign corporation to Switzerland without having to liquidate it if certain conditions are met first. It is, of course, also possible to establish a Swiss branch of a foreign corporation. In either case you should once again refer to your bank or a corporate lawyer in Switzerland for further guidance.

Kommanditaktiengesellschaft (Limited Partnership): This type of incorporation combines elements of both the limited partnership (Kommanditgesellschaft) and the corporation (Aktiengesellschaft). It is used in the case where one or more members of the partnership assume the management of an enterprise with full liability while also accepting additional capital contributions from other members who have limited liability (OR764/765).

The name of a limited partnership firm must include the name of at least one of the partners with unlimited liability and it too must be written into the Commercial Register.

Such a type of corporation is seldom utilized in Switzerland.

Gesellschaft mit beschränkter Haftung (Limited Liability Company): This type of company, the GmbH, is better known in Germany than in Switzerland. It is an association with its own legal personality in which two or more persons or companies participate (OR 772).

The registered capital must be at least 20,000.00 Swiss francs and not more than 2,000,000.00 Swiss francs. A minimum of 50% of this capital must be paid in by the partners at the time of formation. Each partner participates in the capital with a fixed amount and each can be held liable for an amount equal to the total registered capital.

For practical purposes you can see the GmbH as a compromise between a regular corporation and a personal partnership. Like these two forms it too assumes a legal personality once it is entered in the Commercial Register.

Genossenschaft (Co-operative): The co-operative is an association organized along corporate lines and is made up of a variable number of persons or companies. The co-operative has a common goal in the promotion or protection of certain economic interests of its members. The liability of a co-operative is limited to its own assets.

This was a very brief description of the different types of legal business entities existing in Switzerland. The costs of formation and the taxation of the companies once they are in existence varies from canton to canton. As far as costs are concerned there are the fees for entry into the Register of Commerce, the cost of the stamp duty leveled on newly issued shares (2% on the capital stock), the cost of the notarized certificate of incorporation and the expenses for an attorney to coordinate the establishment of your business enterprise. Below we discuss the taxation of Swiss companies.

The Taxation of Companies. Swiss companies are subject to taxes from three sources: the federal tax, the cantonal tax and the municipal tax. The total tax bill is therefore quite dependent on the domicility of the company. While the federal tax is fixed, the cantonal and municipal taxes vary considerably from location to location.

Upon the formation of a Swiss company there is a federal tax of 2% to be paid on the issue price of the share capital. The federal taxes levied against companies once they are in operation is dependent upon whether the company is recognized as an operating company engaged in ordinary business activities or if the company has the character of a holding company. Companies that have the character of holding companies receive favorable tax treatment in Switzerland.

The tax rate on operating companies can not exceed 9.8% of net income. For holding companies this maximum tax rate is reduced by a proportion equal to the portion of the company's gross income which is derived from its holdings.   Thus if a Swiss holding company derives 100% of its income from holdings then it owes no income tax.

The cantonal taxes are quite similar to those of the fedral government. They consist of a tax on both income and on paid in capital plus reserves. Holding companies again are given a fairly substantial relief from capital tax and in most cases are not subject to any income tax from the cantons.

Municipal taxes vary greatly. They utilize the same basic tax base as the cantonal taxes and can vary from a small percentage of the cantonal tax to a multiple of the cantonal tax. Holding companies again are given preferred treatment.

Below we look at the effective cantonal and municipal tax rates for holding companies in various localities in Switzerland":

Canton	Effective tax rate
Aargau	.06% tax on paid in capital, declared reserves and those undeclared reserves taxes as income, with a minimum tax of 300 Swiss francs. Municipal taxes: none
Basle City	.1% on paid in capital as well as on those reserves and other provisions taxed as income upon their formation. Municipal taxes: none.
Bern	.05% on paid in capital and reserves. Municipal taxes: .05% of paid in capital and reserves.

Canton	Effective tax rate
Geneva	.21% on paid in capital and reserves. Municipal taxes: .06% on paid in capital and reserves.
Luzern	.1% on paid in capital. No tax on earnings; no municipal taxes.
Schwyz	.04% to .1% on nominal capital and reserves (progressive tax scale from Sfr. 250,000.00 to capital of more than Sfr. 2,000,000.00). No tax on earnings; no municipal taxes.
Valais	.35% on paid in capital, declared reserves and those undeclared reserves taxed as income. Municipal tax same as tax on capital.
Zug	.15 to .05% (regressive tax scale) on paid in capital. Minimum of 300.00 Swiss francs. No tax on earnings; no municipal taxes.
Zürich	.07% on net assets with capital stock not considered a debt. Municipal tax .9% on same tax base as above for capital tax.

Similar to the holding companies are the so-called domicilary companies in Switzerland. The tax rates they are subject to are very similar to those for holding companies. A domiciliary company does not have an interest of more than 20% in the share capital of other companies (otherwise it would be a holding company) at the same time, although it has legal domicile in a canton, it does not own real estate or transact business there. Typical domiciliary companies would be those owning patents, real estate abroad and generally those companies whose income is derived from transactions concluded abroad.

CHAPTER 22

Liechtenstein Trusts

If you have plans to bring a considerable amount of assets into Switzerland and are keen on preserving your privacy then you should consider establishing a trust or foundation in Liechtenstein. The big advantage is that all the business you do through your Swiss bank can be done in the name of the Liechtenstein firm. In this way you distance yourself once again from having to admit any relations with a Swiss bank.

The Anstalt or Stiftung in Liechtenstein may well be the ultimate means by which to provide investors with discretion. To open such a firm it will be necessary for you to take a trip to Liechtenstein and visit a lawyer there. Your Swiss bank, if you wish, can suggest a lawyer there for you or, if you prefer, you may visit one of the three banks in Liechtenstein, the Liechtensteinische Landesbank, the Bank in Liechtenstein, or Privat Bank. These banks, particularly the latter two, can provide you with assistance in forming an Anstalt or Stiftung in Liechtenstein.

A Stiftung roughly corresponds to what in the English speaking world is known as a charitable foundation. The big difference is that in Liechtenstein the beneficiary of a Stiftung can be a private individual. The Stiftung is endowed with an amount of funds that can be added to at any time. The funds can be used for most any purpose apart from actively engaging in business. It is up to the founder of the foundation to determine how the funds are to be invested.

The Anstalt is similar to a trust. It can hold financial interest in foreign firms and exercise control over them, although the Anstalt itself should not be an operating business.

The minimum amount of capital needed for either firm is 30,000.00 Swiss francs. Just as is the case for a Swiss firm though, this capital can be drawn out after formation of the firm.

Although you are the founder, the head of such a firm for all who might inquire appears to be your Liechtenstein lawyer. It is his name that is entered on all the state documents. There is no way that you are directly linked to the firm. For your security you in turn will have a separate agreement with the lawyer that states he is holding his powers solely in trust for you and that furthermore he will take no action nor make any decisions without your approval. Under Liechtenstein law such a firm must maintain a bank account in Liechtenstein and your lawyer would be required to have signature rights. You can get around this though by instructing the bank in Liechtenstein which is holding the account to take instructions and make payments only when your signature in conjunction with your lawyer's appears on the instructions.

The costs of establishing on Anstalt or Stiftung are a 2% tax based on paid in capital, a deposit fee for documents, an annual tax of .1% on proven capital and reserves and the cost of legal fees. The initial costs for such a firm are about 4,000.00 Swiss francs. Added to this are the yearly fees to the lawyer who is "running" your firm. These charges are about an additional 1,500.00 Swiss francs per year.

CHAPTER 23

Living in Switzerland—Permits and Citizenship

For those who look at Switzerland as a haven, whether economic or political, the thought of living in Switzerland, even on a temporary basis, has considerable appeal. It may not be the most progressive country in the world, but that perhaps is its ultimate attraction. Crime is minimal, the people enjoy the highest per capita income in the world, and organization and efficiency are paramount to the social order. Poverty is nearly non-existent and modern amenities are available to all. On the other hand, compared to their Latin neighbors the Swiss appear rather dull. Generally the Swiss are a suspicious and cautious people; in a social context they are more likely to observe than become involved. As a sociologist recently commented life in Switzerland can be likened to a formal banquet: all that you require is laid out before you but social restraints and custom will prevent you from indulging.

Do not be looking for a paradise and do not expect that you can do anything you want to once in Switzerland. There are no hardships to life in Switzerland but the transition presumes adaptation and if you are not ready to adapt you will not find peace. So before making a decision do consider what life in Switzerland would mean for you. Realize that a move to Switzerland will mean a considerable investment to you both in terms of time and money. The residency and citizenship laws, as we shall see, are very demanding. The Swiss will not give you something for nothing.

I can not describe to you what life in Switzerland is like. To different people it is different things. Your way of life is your affair; visits to Switzerland and careful consideration of your goals may lead you to contemplate a move to Switzerland. If so, the following discussion of residency and citizenship requirements can guide you. It is a complicated and time-consuming affair that deserves careful consideration.

Residency and Work Permits

You can spend up to six months a year in Switzerland without any problems simply by going in as a tourist. Under the law a tourist can spend up to three contiguous months in Switzerland without obtaining any special permission. A tourist can do this twice over a one year period. With very few exceptions do the Swiss require a visa for visits and as you pass through customs you will notice that, as an official practice, they do not even stamp passports.

If you want to reside or work in Switzerland the process becomes more involved. A person who wants to reside in Switzerland will fit into one of the following categories:

Those Wishing to Reside in Switzerland and Not Seeking Employment

By agreeing not to seek employment you must understand that this also excludes you from seeking self-employment and means for all practical purposes that you must be retired. If you are actively engaged in business either in Switzerland or abroad you are not eligible for residency under this category. Furthermore, you must prove to Swiss authorities that you will be financially self-sufficient in Switzerland. You can not have any dependent children living abroad. Your age, or that of your spouse, must be at least 65 years old. Many people who do get residency under these conditions also are able to prove some sort of family ties to Switzerland; although this is not necessarily required, it is a big help. This is probably the easiest means of getting a residency permit, but it is by no means automatic. Cases are considered individually and unless you can show some special reason for wanting to retire in Switzerland your request will meet with considerably delays.

Those Seeking Residency and a Work Permit

It is quite difficult at this time to obtain both a residency and a work permit for Switzerland. This Swiss are very choosy in filling any openings they have in their work force.

Every canton has a quota for foreign workers that is fixed by the federal government. The quota is divided into different fields, for example, health, education, international organizations, etc. In each field a certain number of foreign workers will be allowed in each year. Anyone who is given permission to reside in Switzerland as a full-time worker is granted at first an Aufenthaltsbewilligung (Permit for residency). This entitles the holder to remain at work within the canton for a period of one year at a time. At the end of the year the permit is reviewed and, with almost no exceptions, is renewed for another year.

There is also in each canton a quota for seasonal workers. This number is considerably larger than the number of workers that are given permission to work year round in Switzerland. In Zürich, for example, the quota for seasonal workers is 17,000, for full time year round workers, 1,000 per year. The seasonal workers are given permission to reside in Switzerland from March to December. Their permission must also be renewed each year.

Getting permission to work in Switzerland is difficult but not impossible. Depending on how flexible you are it is suggested you try to obtain residency in one of the less well known cantons. Their quotas are smaller but you have better chance getting into one of them because less people apply.

You should know that it is almost impossible for the self-employed to get a residency permit, but if a Swiss firm or agency vouches for your capabilities and special talents, the process will become much easier. Also, artists, musicians and writers may find residency and citizenship easier to obtain because the quotas in those categories are more flexible.

Once you have an Aufenthaltsbewilligung in a canton you are limited to residency and employment solely in that canton. If after a time you wish to move to another canton you must apply to the canton you wish to move to for an Aufenthaltsbewilligung in that canton. Usually getting a permit to move to another canton

Geneva. The Jardin Anglais on the left bank.

is not too difficult as moves from one canton to another do not fall under the quota system.

As an aside to American businessmen contemplating a move to Switzerland, I urge you to consider your tax situation carefully. While in Switzerland you will not only be paying Swiss taxes but U.S. taxes as well. The U.S. is one of the few countries in the world that taxes according to citizenship rather than residency. Thanks to the double taxation agreement with the Swiss however, Americans can credit the Swiss taxes they pay against their U.S. taxes. If you are not careful though, this will mean you end up paying the higher of the two tax rates. It is another factor to consider if you are thinking of moving.

Turning a Residency Permit into a Citizenship

After having obtained a permit for residency you have taken your first step towards citizenship. As mentioned before the residency permit is renewed every year. At the end of five years it is renewed for two years and so on until you have spent a total of ten years in Switzerland. During these ten years you are allowed intermittent stays abroad which can not total more than three years abroad for each of the last five in Switzerland (the time spent abroad of course does not count toward your citizenship requirement).

After ten years you are granted a Niederlassungsbewilligung (permit to settle). This gives you all the rights a Swiss enjoys except one—you are not a citizen yet. With a Niederlassungsbewilligung you can settle and work anywhere in Switzerland at anytime and without having to apply for permission. After twelve years of residency in Switzerland you are eligible to apply for citizenship.

To be recognized a citizen you must be acceptable to the federal government, the canton, and the Gemeinde (community where you live). Each entity has different requirements. The cantonal and Gemeinde requirements vary from place to place. Basically you have to prove that you have fulfilled your residency requirement of at least twelve years in Switzerland and at least two in the same Gemeinde. To your canton you have to prove that you will not be a financial burden to them and to your community and you must exhibit that you have adapted to the life style and mores of your fellow Swiss. Quite a thorough check is made on your past and on how well you have been able to fit into Swiss life. Police will interview your family and friends and finally a committee of peers from your community will meet to discuss your case. If you are accepted by the federal government, the canton, and the Gemeinde you become a Swiss citizen.* There is a special one-time tax that has to be paid to the Gemeinde and the canton. The tax rates varies from area to area but there is at present a maximum tax rate of 30,000 Swiss francs that you could be assessed.

The process, as you see, is long and exacting, but there are mitigating circumstances possible if you have ties in Switzerland. If, for example, you marry a Swiss woman you only have to wait five years before applying for citizenship; if you are a woman married to a Swiss man you do not have to wait at all. You are automatically a Swiss citizen (not surprising from a country in which women are still not enfranchised in three cantons). There are other mitigating factors; a lawyer in Switzerland can provide the best information for your particular case.

Ultimately though, Swiss citizenship is something you get only if you really want it. There is nothing simple about it and few shortcuts. There is also no such thing as buying a Swiss citizenship. Federal requirements are extremely strict.

To the person who wants to settle in Switzerland: residency, with a bit of luck, is possible; citizenship is something you should not even be thinking about until you are living there.

*You can apply more than once.

CHAPTER 24

The Future of Swiss Banking

The plans and decisions of any industry must be shaped with a sober and practical eye to the future. The rapid expansion of the Swiss banking system in recent years necessitates that the Swiss bankers now make careful judgments if they want to maintain their growth rate in the future. Their success has been largely symptomatic of the unique advantage of Switzerland as a financial center. Whether or not these trends will continue we cannot reliably predict.

In the past Switzerland has financed its economic growth by acting as a clearing house for international funds. Swiss banks would accumulate funds from domestic savings and from foreigners who invested their wealth in Switzerland either for reasons of security or expected financial gain. In turn as the domestic economy could not provide sufficient investment opportunities the Swiss banks found themselves reinvesting these funds abroad. As this has increased we have seen an expansion of Swiss bank foreign operations through the establishment of branches, affiliates and representative offices throughout the world. This process has of course fundamental implications for banking policy. Step by step it is transforming the Swiss banks which only 20 years ago conducted almost all their business from within Switzerland, into enterprises of multinational status.

This new status has brought with it new risks both economic and political. The banks will find themselves cooperating more and more closely with the National Bank in order to avoid these risks. The importance of the National Bank has increased significantly since the advent of "the managed float." The new National Bank Law will give them more of the all encompassing power that they need to do a thorough job. Swiss bankers suspect that over the coming years the National Bank will become more and more involved in the control of the economy. Because of Switzerland's close economic and financial ties with the rest of the world the National Bank will, in addition to supervising the domestic economy, have to be conscious of the external pressures that provide the backdrop for the domestic money and capital markets.

In a recent interview, Franz Leutweiler, the President of the Swiss National Bank, stressed that price stability will continue to be the number one priority of the National Bank when it formulates its monetary policy. Citing the experience of the immediate post World War II era, Leutweiler also stated the National Bank regards stable exchange rates as an essential basis for a successful evaluation of international trade and finance. However, he added, the difficulty of determining the degree of, and therefore the need for, parity connection has convinced the Swiss monetary authorities that exchange rate adjustments were not a suitable instrument of short-term cyclical policy but that they should be employed only in a truly serious disruption of the external equilibrium. We can therefore expect that whenever possible the Swiss will try to avoid direct intervention in the foreign exchange markets and would much rather impose capital controls (as they did early in 1978) to influence the exchange rate.

Another problem that the National Bank will be facing is the fact that the stability of the Swiss franc has prompted both public and private foreign institutions to use the franc as a reserve currency. The Swiss government and the National Bank have vehemently resisted this use of the franc and have tried to prevent it, maintaining that the efficiency of the nation's economy as well as the volume of Swiss francs were far too small for such international functions.

The bankers fear that if the Swiss franc were used as a reserve currency foreign liabilities would thereby be created that, in comparison to the Swiss economy, would be extremely large. These extensive liabilities would constitute a potential source of dangerous disturbances. The money market for Swiss francs would effectively be moved beyond the borders, and the control, of Switzerland. Robert Triffin in an article entitled, "The International Monetary System of the Year 2000" points out that international reserve currencies have many drawbacks in the long run. Admittedly over the short term Switerland could benefit from having the franc used as an international reserve. Just as was once the case with the dollar the Swiss could have balance of payment deficits and finance them by printing more francs for foreigners to hold. In effect the weaker countries would be financing the welfare of the Swiss people. In the long run though such a system must break down. It will entail increasingly precarious forms of financing, subject to continuous negotiation or renegotiation of short and medium term credits whose actual liquidation would in fact provoke widespread default by the debtors. Triffin notes that this feeds a speculative climate "prompting destabilizing movements of funds." He also adds that a major defeat inherent in this system is the disproportionate political power conferred upon the major creditor and reserve-debtor countries (like Switzerland). Their economic might as creators of international reserves would make them instantly politicized in the international arena. The tradition of political neutrality would have to be broken.

This problem of politicization is probably the greatest problem the Swiss and the Swiss banking system will have to deal with in the future. Switerland has only survived as a nation and as a financial center because historically it has been able to find a workable balance between politics and pragmatism. For the future rapid structural transformation of the Swiss economy and of its interrelationships with other countries is threatening this balance.

The enormous inflow of foreign funds and the large investments of Swiss banks abroad is quite out of proportion with the country's real economic resources. Today, for example, the volume of foreign short term assets of Swiss banks is considerably greater than that of the money supply (M_1). The extent of this international interdependence and its growth no longer bears any commensurate relationship either to the country's money or credit system.

When we look back at Switzerland's sound financial tradition and its many advantages as a center for finance and investment, we are tempted to view the future of responsibly managed Swiss banks with unreserved optimism. Unmistakably, however, there looms the danger that banking policy will be faced with a widening dichotomy between what is economically important and what is politically possible. The risks inherent in the growing economic might and international interdependence of the Swiss banks must be carefully considered and controlled in the future. It remains to be hoped that insight into the problem facing the banking industry will grow and that increasing reliance will again be put on those traits that enabled the Swiss people to work their way up, despite their country's dearth of natural resources, to their present prosperity.

Appendix I

Name of bank ....

Liquidity statement on .... 19............

	Francs	Francs

I. Total liabilities pursuant to Art. 12 of IO . . ..

  less

  bank deposits set off pursuant to Art. 17, Par. 1, letter a) . . . .

II. *Principal liabilities* ....

III. *Short-term liabilities* pursuant to Art. 17

  a) Bank deposits, repayable within one month . . . .

  less

  aa) liabilities balanced accord. to Art. 17, Par. 2 . . . .

  bb) liabilities balanced accord. to Art. 17, Par. 1, letter a) . . . .

  b) Sight deposits . . . .

  c) Time deposits, repayable within one month . . . .

  d) 15 percent of savings deposits . . . .

  e) 15 percent of balances in deposit, investment and deposit book accounts . . . .

  f) Bonds and medium-term notes, repayable within one month . . . .

  g) Other liabilities repayable within one month . . . .

  Total ....

	Francs	Francs
IV. *Liquid assets,* pursuant to Art. 15		....
a) Cash on hand		....
b) Giro account deposits with the Swiss National Bank		....
c) Postal checking accounts		....
Total		....

V. *Easily marketable assets,* pursuant to Art. 16

a) Bills, rescriptions, bonds and registered debt certificates that can be discounted with the National Bank . . . .

b) Bonds, rescriptions, bills and registered debt certificates that can be pledged with the National Bank . . . .

c) Balances with other banks repayable within one month . . . .

less

bank deposits balanced pursuant to Art. 17, Par. 1, letter a) . . . .

d) Gold at market price for bullion . . . .

e) Foreign government obligations, prime bankers acceptances and other paper of equal quality of foreign issuers or acceptors, maturing within 3 months . . . .

f) Current account loans covered by bonds that can be pledged with the National Bank . . . .

Total   ....

less

pledged easily marketable assets . . . .

principal easily marketable assets . . . .

VI. Liquid assets (IV) and marketable assets (V) combined . . . .

Appropriate Articles of Swiss Federal Banking Law (Appendix I):

Art. 12

Total liabilities within the meaning of Article 4 of the Law are the liabilities in respect to third parties that are to be shown in the balance sheet and the reserves that must be established for future or doubtful engagements.

Art. 17

1. Short-term liabilities within the meaning of Art. 4 of the Law are:
a) balances of other banks on sight and balances of other banks maturing within one month, provided they are not balanced by corresponding assets;
b) deposits on sight;
c) deposits on time, repayable within one month;
d) 15 percent of the savings deposits;
e) 15 percent of the deposits on deposit book accounts and investment savings book accounts;
f) bonds and medium-term notes repayable with one month;
g) all liabilities maturing within one month shown under other liabilities.

2. Short-term liabilities assumed against the pledging of easily marketable assets (Art. 16, Paragraph 3) may first be deducted.

Art. 15

Liquid assets within the meaning of Art. 4 of the Law are cash holdings and balances on giro and postal checking accounts.

Art. 16

1. Easily marketable assets within the meaning of Art 3 of the Law are:
a) bills, rescriptions, bonds and registered debt certificates which can be discounted with the National Bank;
b) bonds, rescriptions, bills and registered debt certificates which can be pledged to the National Bank;
c) balances with other banks on sight maturing within one month, provided they are not balanced by corresponding liabilities;
d) minted and unminted gold, at most at the market price for gold bullion;
e) bonds of foreign states, prime bankers acceptances and similar foreign paper of equal quality maturing within three months;
f) current account loans and advances covered by assets which can be pledged as collateral with the National Bank.

2. Easily marketable assets that are represented by claims against foreign debtors can be taken into consideration only insofar as it is certain that the payment will either be made in Swiss francs or can be transfered into Switzerland if made by means of a foreign currency.

3. Pledged easily marketable assets must be deducted in the amount in which the credit facilities have actually been utilized.

Appendix II

Liquidity Statement

| 1 | 2 Fr. | Pursuant to Art. 18 the liquid assets must amount to | | Pursuant to Art.19 the liquid assets and the marketable assets must together amount to | |
		In % of the short-term liabilities (column 2) — 3	Francs calculated on column 2 with percentage of column 3 — 4 Fr.	In % of the short-term liabilities (column 2) — 5	Francs calculated on column 2 with percentage of column 5 — 6 Fr.
Of the total liabilities (section II) amounting to Fr. .... the short-term liabilities amount to					
a) up to 15%		6		35	
b) from 15% to 25%		12		52½	
c) from 26% to 35%		24		70	
d) over 35%		36		70	
Total acc. to section III				Minimum amount 6% of total liabilities (section I)	

Available:
Liquid assets acc. to IV
Liquid assets plus easily marketable assets acc. to VI

Art. 18

1. The liquid assets must normally at least amount to:

6 percent of the amount of the short-term liabilities that does not exceed 15 percent of the principal liabilities, plus

12 percent of the amount of the short-term liabilities that does exceed 15 percent but not 25 percent of the principal liabilities, plus

24 percent of the amount of the short-term liabilities that exceeds 25 percent but not 35 percent of the principal liabilities, plus

36 percent of the amount of the short-term liabilities that exceeds 35 percent of the principal liabilities.

2. Principal liabilities consist of total liabilities, less the balances of other banks set off in accordance with Art. 17, Paragraph 1, letter a).

3. These provisions do not apply to finance companies and individual proprietorships within the meaning of Art. 1, Paragraph 2, letter b) of the Law (other than bank-like companies).

Art. 19

1. At any time the liquid and the marketable assets must together amount to at least:

35 percent of the amount of the short-term liabilities that does not exceed 15 percent of the principal liabilities, plus

52½ percent of the amount of the short-term liabilities that does exceed 15 percent but not 25 percent of the principal liabilities, plus

70 percent of the amount of the short-term liabilities that exceeds 25 percent of the principal liabilities.

2. However, the liquid and the marketable assets must together amount to at least 6 percent of total liabilities, with the exception of banks whose assets of more than 60 percent of the balance sheet total consist of domestic mortgage investments, including fixed loans and advances with mortgage security.

3. Principal liabilities consist of total liabilities, less the balances of other banks set off in accordance with Art. 17, Paragraph 1, letter a).

Footnotes

Introduction

[1] Mast, Hans. *Das Schweizerische Bankwesen,* Zürich, 1977, p. 5.

[2] Fehrenbach, T.R. *The Swiss Banks,* New York, 1966, p. 26.

[3] Iklé, Max. *Switzerland: An International Banking and Financial Center,* Stroudsburg, PA, 1972, p. 21.

[4] Fehrenbach, T.R. *The Swiss Banks,* New York, 1966, p. 94.

Chapter Four

[1] From "Die Kleine Anleitung zur Geschäftsführung der Raiffeisen-Vereine 1906", IN *Cooperation at Home and Abroad,* Fay, C.R., London, 1908, p. 42.

Chapter Nine

[1] For a good legal description of tax law in Switzerland refer to: Konauer, Mario. "Tax Information from Switzerland", IN *Tax Law Review, Vol. 30, NYU Law, New York, 1974, pp 47-99. This case is from p. 50.*

[2] The IRS had requested information from a bank about a U.S. citizen (X) who was suspected of tax fraud, pp 70-71, *Tax Law Review,* see above.

[3] Quote of Professor Röpke from: Bieri, Ernst."Das Bankgeheimnis ist nicht gefährdet" IN"Finanz und Wirtschaft" Zürich, May 25, 1977, p. 2.

Chapter Eleven

[1] Quote of Franz Leutweiler in *Der Notenbankausweis,* by Carl Wild, "Neue Zürcher Zeitung" excerpts, Zürich, 1975, p. 2.

[2] Ritzmann, Franz, Zur Revision des Nationalbankgesetzes: Ein Seminarbericht, Bern, 1977, p. 98.

[3] Ibid. p. 99.

[4] Haberler, G., "The Case Against Capital Controls for Balance of Payment Reasons", IN *Capital Movements and Their Control,* Leiden, Netherlands, 1976, p. 74.

Chapter Twelve

[1] As described by the OECD Annual Report on Switzerland, March 1974, pp 24-34.

Chapter Thirteen

[1]Translation of §23 and §34 of the new Austrian Bank Law issued on February 20, 1979:

XIII. Bank Secrecy

§23.   (1) Credit institutions, their partners, board members and employees are not allowed to disclose or make use of any secrets which have been entrusted or made available to them exclusively on the basis of business relationships with clients (Bank secrecy). In case officials of civil authories, during their duties, learn facts underlying bank secrecy, they are bound by their secrecy principles and may be released from them only in cases specified under paragraph 2. The liability to the bank secrecy is not subject to any time restriction.

(2) The obligation to bank secrecy does not exist

1.   in the context of criminal court procedures and of court prosecution of deliberate financial offenses, not including tax irregularities, or

2.   in the context of probate procedures (§98 des Ausserstreitgesetzes (non-litigious civil procedures), RGB1. Nr. 208/1854) or

3.   in case the client explicitly authorizes the disclosure of the secret in writing or

4.   for information of a general nature and common practice in banking regarding the business situation of enterprises, provided the client does not oppose the disclosure of such information.

(3) A credit institution cannot refer to bank secrecy in cases where the disclosure of a secret is required for the determination of the institution's own tax obligations.

§34.   (1) Persons who release or make use of information subject to bank secrecy (§23) in order to procure for themselves or other persons a financial advantage or with the intent of causing disadvantage to other persons will be sentenced to imprisonment for a period of up to one year or with a penalty of up to 360 days court rates.

[2]At present banks, due to new regulations, can no longer hold Swiss francs for you in this manner, but the opportunity may return again.

Chapter Eighteen

[1]from Vontobel & Cie, "Kleines Brevier der Zürcher Börse," 1977, p. 23.

UPDATING ADDENDUM

Each edition of this book will contain an updated addendum.

As this edition goes to press, two important changes have been made by the Swiss National Bank. They both directly affect the investor who is investing in and through Switzerland.

Abolition of the negative interest commission and the limitations on Swiss franc accounts.

Despite my predictions in Chapters 13 and 20, the Swiss National Bank has completely done away with the limitations imposed on foreigners holding accounts in Swiss francs. In late 1979, they reduced the negative interest commission on Swiss franc accounts to 2.5% from 10% on amounts over 200,000 Swiss francs (this we noted). By the year end, however, it was decided to abolish these limitations completely. A foreigner opening a Swiss franc account in Switzerland no longer has a limitation on the amount of Swiss francs he may hold; furthermore, there are no longer any penalties for having more than 100,000 Swiss francs in any one account.

The imposition of the 5.6% turnover tax on gold sales in Switzerland.

For a long time, gold had been so sacred in Switzerland that they dared not even tax it. Despite the fact that the Swiss government may now be trying to cash in on the volatility of the gold market, little will be changed by this tax. As we noted in Chapter 15, when we discussed the turnover tax on silver and other precious metals, the tax is not imposed unless there is actual physical delivery of the metal. So as with silver, gold that is traded on the futures market, in options or through metal accounts, in which the gold is held in duty-free transit zones, is not subject to the tax. You only have to worry about the tax if you physically accept delivery of the gold. For example, if you buy gold coins or gold bullion that you want to take home or put into a safe deposit box, then you are subject to the tax. If you arrange to have the coins or bullion sent to you at an address outside of Switzerland, then you are no longer taxed.

Further changes in banking laws and restrictions are bound to occur. When the Swiss franc starts appreciating against other currencies again, we may well see a re-imposition of limitations on Swiss francs that foreigners may hold. The smart investor, to avoid being adversely affected by such changes should, through his bank, keep apprised of the situation.

All other restrictions that we discussed in Chapter 20 are still in effect. It is, for example, still not possible for a foreigner to hold a fiduciary deposit in Swiss francs despite that limitations on other Swiss franc accounts have been lifted.

INDEX

NOTES

NOTES

NOTES

NOTES

NOTES

NOTES

NOTES

NOTES

ASPEN
The Living Art Company of Aspen

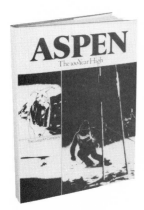

The beauty of Aspen is captured in these beautiful full-color oversize photos of America's most popular, and one of the world's greatest, resort towns. 200 rich, full-color, superb reproductions faithfully portray Aspen in all of its seasons and moods. Year-round majestic landscapes present the seasonal variations offered by this mountain paradise. All of Aspen's sports activities are focussed on, including skiing, mountain climbing, hang gliding, sailing, running the rapids in Kayaks, and Aspen's rich cultural events.

Finally, numerous photos concentrate on one of Aspen's most fascinating attractions, the unique and interesting people who live there. The book successfully captures the unique atmosphere of this favorite vacation spot which annually draws over 1,000,000 visitors from all over the United States. This is the only available hard cover picture book of Aspen.

To order, send $29.95 (plus $1.05 p.&h.) to: BOOKS IN FOCUS. 30 day return privilege.

THE DIAMOND CONNECTION
Antony C. Sutton

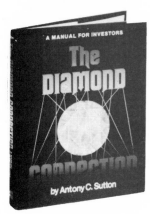

This is the Handbook of diamonds as investments. Economics Professor Antony Sutton presents the facts on all aspects of diamonds, important to investors. The book is designed for the layman and details are given in easily understood language on topics such as the four "C's" of diamond grading. He traces how different sizes and shapes of diamonds perform investmentwise in the market. The questions of how to buy diamonds and where to sell them are covered, as well as the dangers and pitfalls for the unwary. Professor Sutton compares the performance of diamonds during recessions and booms. He goes through the steps of identifying synthetic and simulated diamonds. How the De Beers Cartel markets diamonds and an analysis of its financial strength are given. The future of this monopoly, and the potential for Russian influence on the diamond market are candidly discussed. Finally, whether particular investors should consider investing in diamonds, or not, in the first place, is analyzed.

To order, send $19.95 (plus $1.05 p.&h.) to: BOOKS IN FOCUS. 30 day return privilege.

THE GOLD CLAUSE
Henry Mark Holzer

Gold clauses are contract provisions which protect creditors from depreciating paper money (inflation), so that they receive value rather than paper. This book is the handbook on gold clauses, for all those interested in using them. It contains essays, briefs and court opinions on all major aspects of gold clauses, selected and edited by Professor Holzer. It explains the purpose of gold clauses, their historical use, pre-"New Deal," and discusses the different types of gold clauses, including the Congressional debates, resolutional, judicial aspects, and analysis of court cases.

It then follows the progress of re-legalization of gold ownership and gold clauses and brings the reader up to the present day situation focussing on the important errors to be avoided in drafting gold clauses if they are to stand up in court. This includes the usury laws, retroactivity of the existing clauses, and potential for future repeal.

To order, send $19.95 (plus $1.05 p.&h.) to: BOOKS IN FOCUS. 30 day return privilege.

THE ORATOR
Peter N. Zarlenga

The Orator is a dynamic collection of essays, poems, and methods designed to make the human mind aware of its potential for glory, achievement and joy.

It is a powerful statement of pride in America and in the great new principles of freedom put into effect by our founding fathers. It is also a strong attack on the people and institutions (both secular and philosophical), which have subsequently compromised those freedoms.

The Orator is a book illuminating the concepts of principle, thought, good and evil, achievement, joy, and action. It is a book which has a strong effect on people.

One section presents a distillation of hundreds of years of thought on methods of achievement—four principles which are inspiring, and powerful in their direct simplicity.

To order, send $14.95 (plus $1.05 p.&h.) to: BOOKS IN FOCUS. 30 day return privilege.

THE SWISS BANKING HANDBOOK
Robert Roethenmund

This is the complete handbook on Swiss banks for investors, corporations, and all who invest, travel or transact business internationally.

It gives a complete description of the Swiss banking system including: the Swiss franc; the National Bank; and the Giro Systems; the background of Swiss secrecy and independence; and the cantonal political system.

On the practical side, the book describes various types of banking accounts and services and exactly how to use them. For example, precious metals accounts, commodity accounts, margin accounts, various currency accounts, stock accounts, as well as standard checking/savings accounts.

The book describes the working of the Swiss stock market including its unique margin and payment requirements and the tax haven aspects of Switzerland including various types of corporations, their tax status, how such companies are formed, and which cantons offer the most advantageous situations.

Finally, the rules for Swiss residency, work permits and Swiss citizenship are described, debunking the idea that any of these are easy to get, or can be bought.

To order, send $19.95 (plus $1.05 p.&h.) to: BOOKS IN FOCUS. 30 day return privilege.

NAMIBIA
Prof. Mbrumba Kerina

This is a primary source book on Namibia. It is the only contemporary and thorough book of its kind; a work which will be needed by all African Studies departments; all substantial libraries and many others, as Namibia's independence moves to center stage in the drama of Southern Africa. Since Prof. Kerina was at the center of much of South West Africa's history, he brings a rare authority to the subject. The backgrounds of the various ethnic groups in South West Africa are described and their characteristics analyzed. The history of the country is given, from the time of the German occupation to the 1970's, including details of the decimation of the Herreros in the German-Herrero War, and profiles of Black leadership and ideals during these periods. The author discusses the major mining concerns in the territory, and presents principles of ownership to guarantee property rights during the transition to independence.

Prof. Kerina is the original founder of the South West African People's Organization (SWAPO) and remained its guiding light until it was taken over by Russian influence, at which time he resigned. He is responsible for coining the name Namibia, now accepted as the new name for what used to be South West Africa.

To order, send $19.95 (plus $1.05 p.&h.) to: BOOKS IN FOCUS. 30 day return privilege.

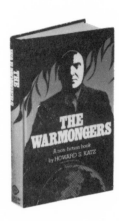

THE WARMONGERS
A Non-Fiction Book
Howard S. Katz

They started World War I.
They engineered World War II.
They are moving the world toward war now!

Who they are, *how* they have operated, and above all *why* they are warmongers, is carefully documented in this brilliant analysis.

THE WARMONGERS re-examines *history* and discovers a distressing link between the creation of paper money and major wars. Detailed facts expose a fascinating and frightening intrigue in which bankers, big business and government create wars to increase their power and wealth.

THE WARMONGERS analyzes the *present* and uncovers a consistent trail of actions on the highest level, designed to lead the U.S. into major war.

THE WARMONGERS projects the *future*, convincingly predicting that America and China will be fighting Russia and Japan; tells what major policy shifts must occur; and explains why 1981 and 1985 are the most likely years for the U.S. to be brought into the war.

THE WARMONGERS is a non-fiction book.

To order, send $11.95 (plus $1.05 p.&h.) to Books In Focus. 30 day return privilege.

CONFLICT OF MINDS
Jordan K. Ngubane

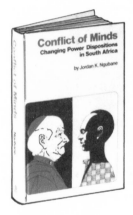

Conflict of Minds is a brilliant redefinition of the South African Crisis in terms of two conflicting philosophies of life, rather than a racial struggle.

Ngubane shows how the Sudic philosophy of Africa, and attitude toward the person evolved from ancient Egyptian theology, being passed on from generation to generation through the oral tradition; and he traces it to present day Zulu philosophy.

Conflict of Minds is the first written presentation of this philosophy ever, and therefore represents a major cultural achievement. It is a clear demonstration that there is a unifying world view throughout Africa, and that contrary to popular belief this view is in respects actually in advance of the Judeo-Christian structure. This has implications for that structure which cannot be ignored.

ABOUT THE AUTHOR:

Conflict of Minds represents a labor of 10 years for Mr. Jordan K. Ngubane. During this period he has been in exile from his home and people in the Zulu areas of South Africa. Living in Washington, D.C. and lecturing at Howard University, Jordan has maintained an objective attitude and has remained very much in touch with Black leadership within South Africa.

This is Jordan Ngubane's fifth book. He was the editor of a South African Black newspaper for eight years and was the correspondent for Mahatma Ghandi's newspaper. He has written 10 articles for the McGraw-Hill New Encyclopedia of World Biographies.

To order, send $10.95 (plus $1.05 p.&h.) to Books In Focus. 30 day return privilege.

IMMORTAL LIGHT OF GENIUS
The Flight Organization

In this volume you will find the immortal light of genius at its moments of greatest inspiration discovering truth, creating beauty, moving Humanity to fulfill its dream of Glory . . . freedom, achievement and joy.

Touch this blue fire of genius, this immortal light, this glory, with your mind and with your heart and it will set fire to your spirit.

The immortal light of genius is the energy for life.

To order, send $5.95 (plus $1.05 p.&h.) to Books In Focus. 30 day return privilege.

POWER IS OURS
M. Gatsha Buthelezi

Buthelezi Speaks on the Crisis in South Africa

"The speeches of *BUTHELEZI* provide a tremendous source of material . . . on the South African Problem . . . The reader will gain new insight as he is led by this gifted mind and articulate person . . . It's extremely important that (he) is heard and understood . . . he has earned the right to be heard."

    Rev. Leon H. Sullivan
    Director, General Motors Corporation
    Minister, Zion Baptist Church
    Author of the Sullivan Code of Ethics for American Companies operating in South Africa

An epic struggle is unfolding in South Africa—a struggle destined to affect the entire world. At the forefront of this movement a leader has arisen.

A *MAN* whose existence cannot be ignored by the South African or world media;

A *MAN* too powerful to be dealt with in typical Apartheid fashion;

A *MAN* who combines rare qualities of leadership, intellect, organization, and courage;

A *MAN* whose hour has come.

This man is Gatsha Buthelezi. He is the leader of 5,000,000 Zulu people in South Africa; he is the Chairman of INKATHA and of the South African Black Alliance.

This book contains some of his most powerful speeches, covering every topic of importance in the South African dilemma. As you read through its pages you will be drawn into Gatsha's struggle and life, and will share his moment in history.

Topics are indexed by a unique "Idea Index."

To order, send $12.95 (plus $1.05 p.&h.) to Books In Focus. 30 day return privilege.

RUDEBARBS
Randall Hylkema

RUDEBARBS are cartoons with a message! Some of the funniest economic, political, and social lampoons ever created; thanks to the genius of Randy Hylkema. Guaranteed to have you in stitches or your money refunded.

To order send $5.95 ($1.05 p.&h.) to Books In Focus. 30 day return privileges.

SOUTH AFRICA: SHARP DISSECTION
Christiaan Barnard

Christiaan Barnard, the world renowned South African heart surgeon speaks his mind on the dilemma in his country, and other trouble spots in Africa.

"In an unquestionably heartfelt expression of his views as a white Afrikaner proud of his heritage and land, he asserts his reasoned opinion that apartheid should be ended immediately—for practical as well as moral reasons."—PUBLISHERS WEEKLY (review)

Here is a view of South Africa for the reader who wants to form his own judgment, a view based on practical knowledge of the situation as analyzed by an intelligent mind. As the situation there threatens to explode and intrude more and more into our lives, concerned persons will want to understand this viewpoint.

To order, send $8.80, hardback (plus $1.05 p.&h.) to Books In Focus. 30 day return privilege.

ENERGY: THE CREATED CRISIS
Antony C. Sutton

YOUR TAXES ARE GOING UP; YOUR ELECTRIC AND GAS BILLS ARE COSTING MORE; AND THE GOVERNMENT IS TELLING YOU TO USE YOUR AIR CONDITIONER LESS IN THE SUMMER—WHY?
FOR AN ENERGY CRISIS THAT DOESN'T EXIST

In ENERGY: THE CREATED CRISIS, Antony C. Sutton confirms the suspicion long held by many Americans that the energy "crisis" is a hoax perpetrated on the American people by big government aided and abetted by big business.
Inside are the details on:

- *America's present energy reserves—enough for the next 2000 years*
- *How and why the U.S. government works to obstruct energy development*
- *Which huge multi-national oil companies are most politically active in supporting the government's efforts to encourage the energy "crisis"—and why*
- *Nuclear energy—far cheaper and safer than oil, coal and gas*
- *The Carter energy plan—a taxation plan in disguise*
- *The ruling elite—who they are and how they're working against you*

To order, send $10.95 (plus $1.05 p.&h.) to Books In Focus. 30 day return privilege.

HONEST MONEY NOW!
Howard S. Katz

DONT TREAD ON ME

SELECTED ESSAYS By HOWARD S. KATZ

Arise then ye freemen, use liberty's hand
And drive this vile paper from liberty's land,
And let the gold dollar be coin for the poor
And circulate freely to every man's door,
Awake up to freedom and not be controlled,
Submit not to bankers to pocket your gold.

100 years ago it was common knowledge that gold money was in the interest of the average citizen and that paper money served the interests of bankers and charlatans. History shows that the struggle between paper money and hard money had been the dominant political issue in the United States until World War I.
Today, the fight between hard money and paper money is again becoming the primary political issue of our time.
Honest Money Now! is the first shot fired in the action-phase of this struggle. In **The Paper Aristocracy**, Howard Katz explained why the gold standard was essential to our nation. In **The Warmongers**, he showed how the paper money interests were moving our nation toward war. In **Honest Money Now!**, he explains how the Gold standard can be achieved now, and what you ought to be doing about it!

To order, send $3.95 (plus $1.05 p.&h.) to Books In Focus. 30 day return privilege.

THE PAPER ARISTOCRACY
A Simple Explanation of What is Happening to Your Money
Howard S. Katz

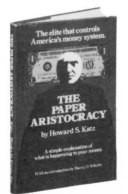

Katz has written a new classic as important to the development of economic thought as Adam Smith's *Wealth of Nations*, or Marx's *Das Kapital*. For in this book Katz carefully documents the development of a powerful elite, which through the mechanisms of paper money, has come to control the economies of Nations. This group, which Katz calls the paper aristocracy, reaps unearned benefits from this control at the expense of the people. For the first time ever, economics is not viewed as a cold science, but is evaluated within a moral framework. What's more, Katz does it in clear language easily understood by the layman or student.
The Paper Aristocracy represents a major revolution in economic thinking. Howard Katz deserves the praise and thanks of all honest men. Order his book now.
"Your presentation is about the most penetrating and stimulating of any I have read in years. You are absolutely right—paper money inflation makes the poor poorer and the rich richer."—ELGIN GROSECLOSE, PH.D., Institute for Monetary Research, Inc., Washington, D.C.

To order, send $7.95 (plus $1.05 p.&h.) to Books In Focus. 30 day return privilege.

SPECIAL DISCOUNTS TO READERS

The following quantity discounts are available to readers who want to help spread the message of this book. (The same discount applies to all books available through Books In Focus).

10 copies	20%
25 copies	30%
50 copies	40%
100 or more	45%

Add 25¢ per book for postage and handling. New York residents add sales tax also. Mail your order and check to: BOOKS IN FOCUS, P.O. Box 3481, Grand Central Station, New York, N.Y. 10017.

■■

To Order Books

Send The Following Information:
(You can send this sheet or photocopy it)

Book Title(s)	Quantity	Cost

Name: _____

Address: _____

City: _____ State: _____

ZIP: _____

Total quantity: _____

Total Cost: _____

Minus % Discount: _____

Plus Postage: _____

Total Due: _____

☐ American Exp. ☐ BankAmericard/VISA ☐ Master Chg.

Account number _ _ _ _ _ _ _ _ _ _ _ _ _ _ _ _

Please give Bank No. (if Master Charge). Expiration date (all cards) or valid date (if Amer. Exp.)

_____ _____ _____ _____

Mo. Yr.

_____

Signature

Send your personal check or money order payable to:

Books In Focus, Inc.
P.O. BOX 3481
GRAND CENTRAL STATION, New York 10017